In Search of RAINBOWS

A daughter's story of loss, hope, and redemption

SUSAN LANDEIS

Copyright 2019 Susan Landeis
Trade paperback ISBN: 978-0-578-58533-8
Printed in the United States of America
Design by Asya Blue

*"In the garden of memory, in the place of dreams…
that is where you and I shall meet."*

In loving memory of my mother, Arlene.

Disclaimer

This book is a memoir. It reflects the author's present recollections of experiences over time. Some names, places, and characteristics have been changed, some events have been compressed, and some dialogue has been recreated. Statements made in this book about Parkinson's disease, dementia, or any other condition or disease is strictly the author's own personal opinion unless otherwise stated. The information contained in this book is advisory only and is not intended to replace sound clinical judgment or individualized patient care. Any outside resource mentioned in this publication is intended for informational purposes only. The author disclaims all warranties, whether expressed or implied.

Table of Contents

Disclaimer i
Introduction 1
Chapter 1 *Yesterday's child.* 5
Chapter 2 *Growing pains* 13
Chapter 3 *A family of my own* 21
Chapter 4 *A devastating diagnosis.* 31
Chapter 5 *Nebraska bound* 37
Chapter 6 *The perfect gift* 43
Chapter 7 *The love letter.* 47
Chapter 8 *The girl with the ponytail.* 51
Chapter 9 *Packing up again.* 57
Chapter 10 *A new beginning.* 63
Chapter 11 *Learning about Lewy.* 69
Chapter 12 *The odd couple* 75
Chapter 13 *Rock around the clock.* 81
Chapter 14 *Strike three!.* 85
Chapter 15 *For everything there is a season* 91
Chapter 16 *Diamonds are forever.* 99
Chapter 17 *Full circle.* 105
Chapter 18 *Swept away* 111
Chapter 19 *All things are possible.* 117
Chapter 20 *Between worlds.* 123
Chapter 21 *Going home.* 127
Chapter 22 *Jason Street* 133
Chapter 23 *Picking up the pieces* 141
Chapter 24 *Putting the pieces together.* 149
Epilogue *Moving forward.* 155
Appendix A *Parkinson's disease* 159
Appendix B *What is Lewy body dementia?* 163
Appendix C *Caregiving.* 167
References 171
Acknowledgments 173
About the Author 175

INTRODUCTION

Every family has a unique story to tell. Families usually consist of people who love and care for one another, even during hard times. They provide an anchor that keeps us from drifting too far away. There are no perfect families in this world, and every relationship has struggles and dynamics to overcome. Mother-daughter relationships may be the most complex of them all. The relationship I had with my mother was no exception. My journey began after my mother was diagnosed with Parkinson's disease and dementia. To find peace and healing after my mother died, I had to go back to the beginning to find the answers I so desperately needed. Throughout my life, I saw only one side of her, the part that was my mother. It was important for me to understand who she was as a person, a human being, and a woman with a past.

After her death, I discovered more than I ever could have imagined. I found the strength to forgive, compassion for the person she was, and faith in my own future. She was a lost soul in this world. I am convinced that our minds are powerful forces. Our thoughts shape who we are. And when turned inward, they have the power to cause irreversible damage, even disease. I understand this is a controversial subject, and it is through my experience that I have learned it is possible to become what we believe ourselves to be, in some cases including illness.

Anyone who has ever had the experience of caring for a loved one with dementia or any other cognitive disease knows firsthand how devastating it can be. The person you once knew is no longer there. No matter your relationship with them, good or bad, it is forever changed. In the case of my mother, she became a different person altogether. It was like meeting someone brand new. As the disease progressed, she was able to "forget" all the reasons why she was so unhappy, and her original self slowly emerged. Some might call it a gift or even a second chance. Either way, I was given an opportunity to have a different kind of relationship with her at the end.

My life experience as a family caregiver was, and still is, the single most challenging chapter in my life. Caring for someone who doesn't necessarily care for you is a bag of mixed emotions that I struggled with every single day. It left me with a very difficult choice to make. I could either turn my back on the situation or take the risk and change the course of our lives. I will always thank God that I chose the latter because it was also the most rewarding chapter. I learned to rebuild the crumbling foundation of what was once a family and discovered how liberating forgiveness could be. But as much as caregiving has taught me, those lessons came at a very high price.

When I quit working to care for both of my parents, everything about my life changed. Before long I started to miss my job, my co-workers, and my professional life. Soon, my so-called friends who promised to keep in touch stopped calling. I no longer had anything in common with them, and I kept more to myself. Even my relationships with other family members, especially my brother, became strained. I felt lost and alone as I struggled to navigate strange and unfamiliar territory. I was stressed out, overwhelmed, and perpetually exhausted. As time went on, I lost more and more of myself to the demands of caregiving. My daily routine now revolved around my parent's care, and there was little time left for the things I used to enjoy and once took for granted. Before I knew it, my life had completely changed.

One day, I was sitting with my dad in the waiting room at the doctor's office when I noticed other "grown children" who also cared for their parents. It suddenly occurred to me that there were others out there like me. Later that evening, I did a search on the Internet for caregiver support groups. I was amazed at all the information I found! I decided to join a few of them and soon started meeting new people. My heart ached as I listened to some of their stories. Most were either burned out, at their wits' end, or just barely surviving their assumed roles in an uncertain, ever-changing world.

I began to feel a close bond as we shared our fears, experiences, and advice. It felt so good to have something in common with others again. I soon realized that I had become a part of a growing population of people known as "caregivers." It was almost like being part of a secret society! Who knew that the act of caring for your loved ones actually had a name? I thought about the many ways people care for their family members and probably don't even realize they are caregivers!

Before long, I was meeting some very special people that are still, and always will be, dear to my heart. I discovered a strong community of people who, like me, had made the difficult decision to care for their family.

As a result of all this, I have come to the conclusion that sometimes it is necessary to completely lose oneself in order to find oneself again. I believe that God gives us who and what we need in our lives so we can become whole again—if we are willing to accept it. When we embrace our ultimate wisdom, we learn to dance with life. This is neither a sad nor tragic story. It is one of growth, possibilities, and hope!

I'm sharing my personal story in the hope that others may find comfort, perhaps a new perspective, or just the common understanding that we all share many struggles as families and human beings. No life situation is ever so difficult that it cannot be overcome with faith, whatever your belief system. On this very personal journey, I have discovered the power of love, healing, and forgiveness. This experience was, and forever will be, life-changing.

CHAPTER 1

Yesterday's child

I shifted in my seat and rolled down the window slightly as we approached the entrance of the cemetery. It was a sunny, crisp fall day, and I had always loved this time of year. As we drove further up the hill, I couldn't believe how much the area had grown since I had been here last spring. The beautiful VA national cemetery where my mother was buried had continued to expand since the day she was laid to rest, almost six years earlier.

I marveled at how I still felt apprehension in the pit of my stomach each time I visited my mother. Even though she was now gone from this world, my body reacted the same way it always had for as far back as I can remember. I placed the flowers in front of my mother's grave and stood up to admire them. I gazed at the words on the headstone. Her death still felt unreal to me. As I ran my fingers over the chiseled words, Gone Home, I suddenly remembered why we chose those words for the inscription. Small details can dredge up a lifetime of memories. Even after nearly six years, I still struggled to understand my relationship with my mother. But to grasp the complexity of it all, it would be necessary to go back to the very beginning.

I lived with my parents in the city of Bismarck, the capital of North Dakota. In 1966, I had just turned three when they bought their first house on a quiet little cul-de-sac. Both of my parents took great pride in their new home. While my mother planted flowers and decorated, my father painted all the rooms and fenced in the back yard. I can still recall my bedroom with cotton-candy-pink walls, white furniture, and pink and white ruffled curtains.

I was an inquisitive child with light blonde hair, green eyes, and a bashful smile. I had a definite stubborn streak and was known to be strong-willed at times. I took after my father's side of the family and was rather tall for my age and rail thin. My mother always pointed out that I was much too skinny and tried her best to "fatten" me up. Even though my mother still had a lovely figure, she had a tendency to gain weight more easily because of her shorter stature and always felt self-conscious about it. Due to my genetics, however, I continued to remain thin, much to her disappointment. She never hid the fact that it embarrassed her, claiming that everyone must think that she couldn't afford to feed her family properly.

My mother, Arlene, was a beautiful woman with chestnut-brown hair and ice-blue eyes. She worked as a beautician before marriage, and always took great care with her appearance. She was a stay-at-home mom, but she liked to look her best and always wore makeup and styled her hair nicely, especially before going out. She dressed casually, but always tastefully. I used to love the musky smell of her perfume, and the way it lingered in the room. My mother liked to surround herself with lovely things. It was just as important to her that our home and family looked picture-perfect as that she herself did. There were silk drapes on the windows, glass knick-knacks on polished wood surfaces, and upholstered furniture throughout the house. It was not overly fancy, but more of an understated elegance. She came from a poor, dysfunctional family. Her mother did her best to raise seven children, but over time, became bitter and emotionally distant. Her alcoholic father worked as a mechanic, often drinking away his meager earnings.

My own father, Cliff, better known as "Jack," was quite different. He had a promising career as a civil engineer, and later became a Master Sergeant for the Army National Guard. He was kind, gentle, and a good provider. He had a calm, easygoing way about him that made one feel at ease. My father was a handsome man with broad shoulders and sandy brown hair, warm smile, and green eyes, just like mine. He had good old-fashioned values, and everyone liked and respected him. My mother seemed to have it all, a beautiful home and a loving husband and family.

Early in their marriage, about two years before I was born, my mother gave birth to a son three days after Christmas. His name was Jason. He came into this world much too early and passed away soon after he was born. I believe this set the stage for much of my mother's feelings of sadness, failure, and depression. She never forgot this first child. At times she would talk about him and what might have been. At other times, the subject was taboo. It was difficult for me to understand as a little girl. But what I did understand was that I had a big brother who watched over me. And he lived in heaven!

I was always very close to my father, but any attention he lavished on me made my mother angry and jealous. I think he tried to make up for what she wouldn't or wasn't capable of giving me, but sadly, it just made the situation worse. It was never any secret that my mother and I were not close. As far back as I can remember, I knew that our relationship was lacking something, especially warmth and affection. We were not like other mothers and daughters.

I used to envy the children I saw on television shows and wished my mother and I could be more like them. She could seem bright and cheery one moment, cold and aloof the next. She was often critical of everyone around her, always looking for someone to blame for her unhappiness. I was usually the one she blamed. It took a toll on me and affected not only my childhood but much of my adulthood as well. I struggled with deep-rooted feelings of unworthiness and felt incapable of being loved. It took me years to figure out that I wasn't the problem. My mother was a broken person.

Even though there weren't many pleasant childhood memories of her and me together, there is one that stands out in my mind. I must have been about five years old, and she had taken me to a nearby park. As she stood at the bottom of the slide waiting to catch me, I surprised her with a flower and told her that I loved her. I saw the look of surprise, and quickly noticed there were tears in her eyes. She gave me a big hug and softly whispered, "I will always love you!" There was a feeling of warmth and tenderness that I longed for, years after that day faded away.

My father often spent long days at the office, and my mother withdrew and always seemed depressed. I would usually find her lying on the couch or in her bedroom with the door half closed. She would say she didn't feel well and preferred to be left alone. Since I loved to play outdoors, I took refuge in the huge empty lot right beside our house. There was lots of tall grass and wildflowers that were even taller than me! It didn't look like much, but to a small child, it was a magical land limited only by my imagination. I would spend hours there playing with bugs, picking flowers, building forts, and making mud pies. It truly was a child's paradise!

Almost five and a half years after I was born, my mother gave birth to another son. On a cold stormy night in December, my little brother Shawn came into the world. I was over the moon at the prospect of having a sibling. I finally had a brother that I could see, touch, and play with! Both of my parents were very proud, and I knew my dad was hopeful that this would help my mother find happiness again.

My paternal grandmother came and stayed with us for several weeks to help with the new arrival. There was a feeling of celebration in the house when people came by to visit and brought gifts. My dad even handed out cigars to all the men. I simply adored my grandmother and enjoyed spending time with her! She read all my favorite stories and we baked cookies together. Everything seemed to be taking a positive turn, at least for a little while.

After my grandmother left us, the house felt lonely, and I missed her terribly. As soon as I would get home from school, my mother would immediately shush me so I wouldn't wake my baby brother. I wanted so badly to tell her about my day, but she always insisted that I talked too loudly. I soon gave up and realized it was just easier to play quietly in my room until dinner time. I was scared of making her angry and upset. She had a quick temper, and I learned how to become invisible when she was having a bad day.

On the weekends when my father was home, he and I would spend time together, so my mother could rest while my brother napped. I always loved these outings with my dad. He was a history buff, and we would visit museums, parks, or historical landmarks. I soon learned to appreciate the importance of our history, almost as much as he did! I always felt like it was our special day, just the two of us. We often stopped at a little corner store on the way home and my dad would buy my favorite candy, and if I was really lucky, I even got a comic book!

Late the following spring, when the school year was almost over, it became clear that having me underfoot was, in fact, more than my mother could handle. It was decided that it would be best if I stayed with my paternal grandparents for the summer. My grandparents lived on a farm just outside of a small town called Merricourt. It was a small farming community where everyone knew each other, and my grandparents proudly introduced me to everyone we saw. I loved everything about their home, and I felt safe and welcome there. It was a typical farmhouse surrounded by fruit trees and lilac bushes. There was even a big red barn that could be seen from several miles away. My grandmother had a green thumb, and there were beautiful plants and colorful flowers everywhere. She even had a flower garden in the yard with lilies, hydrangeas, and beautiful rose bushes. I remember waking up to the scent of fresh flowers drifting in through my bedroom window. Life with them was relaxed and carefree, and time seemed to stand still. I enjoyed the attention my grandparents lavished on me, and I secretly wished I could stay forever.

My grandmother was a lovely woman with brown sparkling eyes, a warm smile, and salt and pepper hair. She was a wonderful cook and there were always mouth-watering aromas coming from the kitchen. My grandfather was an older version of my father, with similar personality and less hair. He had a deep voice and a slight drawl that hinted at his Southern roots. He knew how to tell a good story, and his belly laugh was contagious.

One afternoon late that summer, my father called and said they would be coming to take me home the following weekend. Summer was coming to an end, and I would be starting school again soon. When my grandmother broke the news to me, I told her that I didn't want to go home and begged to stay a little longer. She just smiled, gave me a big hug, and promised I could come back again soon. The week flew by, and on the last morning, I lingered in bed a little longer than usual. I slowly got dressed and neatly made my bed, fluffing the feather pillow and straightening the soft white chenille bedspread. I felt sad as I looked around the bedroom with the pale green walls and lacey curtains that I had come to think of as my own.

When I finally made my way into the kitchen, my grandmother greeted me with my favorite breakfast: cinnamon toast and hot cocoa, with extra marshmallows! Afterword, we packed my suitcase and waited for my parents to arrive. As I sat down on the front porch steps, I noticed a dust cloud in the distance on the gravel road that led to my grandparents' farm. I knew it was my parents. My stomach tightened as the image grew closer.

A few minutes later, the family station wagon pulled up in front of the house. My father stepped out of the car first. He gave me a big smile as I ran toward him and lifted me into a big bear hug. My mother gave me a quick kiss on the cheek, and immediately noticed my hair, which had grown much longer over the summer. With an annoyed expression on her face, she looked up at my grandmother who was standing behind me and asked, "Why is her hair so unkempt?" Before my grandmother could respond, my mother rushed me inside and twisted my unruly blonde hair into a tight ponytail. After that, she insisted that I change my clothes and put on something "decent" before we left for the drive back home. I could tell by the look on my grandmother's face that she did not agree with my mother's finicky ways. They were two very different women!

The first week after I returned home, my mother took me shopping for school clothes and new shoes. Instead of feeling excited, all I wanted to do was go back to my grandparents' farm. I longed for the warm summer days, running through the fields and helping my grandma pick chokecherries, plums, and apples in the orchards for canning and making jam. I missed my grandpa and the way he made me laugh. I was happy there. I had blossomed with their love and acceptance. Even though we still came to visit on weekends and most holidays, there was always a house full of aunts, uncles, and cousins, and I missed spending time alone with my grandparents. As they grew older, the visits happened less often—especially after my grandfather passed away suddenly, when I was twelve. Things were never quite the same again.

CHAPTER 2

Growing pains

As the years went on, life got harder as my mother became more unstable. There would be nasty arguments and cruel words between us. She always seemed to be looking for a fight. She even went as far as telling me that I wasn't her "real" daughter, and would constantly threaten to send me away when I talked back, or tried to defend myself. Her physical state suffered as well. She often complained of debilitating headaches and earaches. She saw doctors and specialists, but no one could find anything wrong with her, so they sent her home with painkillers and an assortment of other medications. When those ran out, she would often choose to self-medicate.

It was not unusual for her to pack a bag and leave for several days, then come back home as if nothing had ever happened. It used to frighten me, and I always felt that it was somehow my fault whenever she left. I still recall one such afternoon, when I arrived home from school and was surprised to find the door locked. I knew where the spare key was, so I let myself in. As I walked into the kitchen, the house felt eerily quiet. I continued down the hall that led to my bedroom and as I passed by my parent's room, I suddenly noticed that my mother's clothes were strewn all over the bed. When I saw the open closet with empty hangers, I realized she was gone.

I felt a wave of panic, and I desperately thought of all the reasons why my mother would just leave without telling us. I suddenly remembered the last time she was angry at me. It was just three days earlier after she yelled at me to clean my room. I angrily sassed back at her. Could she still be mad at me? I suddenly felt scared, and I wondered if my dad knew she was gone. Just then, I heard the front door close and the sound of my brother's voice. My father had picked up Shawn from the daycare center, and I could tell by his worried expression that he already knew my mother had left. When he explained that she was visiting relatives, he avoided my eyes and I knew he wasn't telling the truth.

My father was unusually quiet that evening and I helped him make dinner, and later tucked Shawn into bed. He was only four and cried when he realized his mother was gone. By the end of the weekend, she suddenly returned as if we should have been expecting her. Even though Shawn was overjoyed to have his mother back, all I felt was guilt, confusion, and fear that she would leave again. My dad continued to stand by her, but we all suffered as a family.

I had just turned eleven the summer my parents announced that we were moving to a new house across town. Part of me was excited, but what really made it seem wonderful was my mother's sudden change of mood. She was cheerful and happy for the first time in months! Even though moving to a different neighborhood and going to a new school felt daunting, I found myself looking forward to it, imagining that life would be different now.

The new house was larger than our old one and had many nice features that included a big fireplace in the living room and a cozy, country-style kitchen. My room had bright orange shag carpeting, which was very much the style in the 1970s. I loved it, and my mother let me decorate my room with other bright accents to match! I remember spending a relaxing afternoon with her, paging through the Sears catalog and picking out new curtains, bedspread, and pictures for the walls. Once we settled into our new home, my mother wanted to change everything. She bought new furniture, painted the walls, and had new carpeting and floors installed. My father didn't seem to mind as long as she was happy. But eventually the excitement wore off, and she started to slip back into her old ways.

That fall, I started my first year in middle school. I was extremely nervous and didn't know any of the other kids. One day I was in the school cafeteria, waiting in a long lunch line. Even though I felt shy, I decided to strike up a conversation with the girl in front of me. She had strawberry blonde hair and a warm, friendly smile. She told me her name was Robin, and she lived in my neighborhood, only a few blocks from my house. We had lunch together that day and soon after, became the very best of friends.

As my mother's moods became more upsetting, I began spending more time at Robin's house. I rarely had friends over because my mother would usually embarrass me with one of her outbursts. It always ended with my friend leaving and me feeling humiliated and angry. Later, when I would question her about it, she would try and convince me that she had done me a favor and tell me that friends could never be trusted. It always seemed as though my mother were trying to sabotage my relationships, especially with my father and friends. She even gave away my pets while I was at school.

One afternoon, I came home to find my beloved dog, Rusty, missing. I called his name, and when he didn't come, I asked my mother where he was. She said she didn't know, and ignored my desperate pleas to help find him. Later that day, my dad gently explained that Rusty had an accident on the rug, and my mother took him to the pound. I was heartbroken. She was obviously the one I couldn't trust!

As winter approached, the temperatures turned bitter cold. One afternoon, I arrived home from school to find my brother, Shawn, sitting against the side of the house, crying. When I asked him why he was crying, he pointed to the shattered glass window on the garage door. He explained that our mother wasn't home, and the door was locked so he couldn't get in. We finally managed to get inside the garage, where we sat and waited for over an hour. My poor brother admitted that he was angry for being left outside and had broken the window with his school bag.

Eventually, both my mother and father came home, but neither one seemed to notice our distress, let alone the broken window. It was obvious that something was terribly wrong! That evening, my parents were unusually quiet. They barely spoke to Shawn and me or each other. I assumed they must have had a bad fight, and I eventually went to bed.

The next morning, I noticed that my father had stayed home from work. He was sitting quietly in the kitchen, and my mother was still in bed. I thought he was ill, and quickly finished getting ready for school. Just as I was leaving he quietly said, "Try and have a good day." I thought it was a little odd, but I shrugged it off and continued out the door.

Later that morning at school, the student counselor pulled me out of my fourth-period class. He had a strange, almost pained look on his face as he dropped a bombshell on me. He explained to me very gently that I could no longer live with my parents. My father had moved out of the house, and my mother would not allow me to live there with her. I could feel my face grow pale as I struggled to understand his words, but nothing was making any sense. The counselor patiently answered my questions as best he could and told me that Shawn would stay with my mother, and my father would be in touch with me soon. I was then instructed to pick up my suitcase in the principal's office after school. I would be staying with another student's family who had graciously offered to take me in.

Even though I was in complete disbelief, I tried my best to absorb all this information as I walked back to class. Suddenly my head was spinning, and I couldn't breathe. I felt sick and ran into the girl's bathroom to throw up. Eventually, I pulled myself together as best I could and rejoined my class. I must have looked as sick as I felt because several of the kids, including the teacher, asked if I was all right. Somehow, I managed to get through the rest of that day.

After school, I stopped by the principal's office to retrieve my suitcase and meet the student whose family would be taking me in. The girl's name was Stephanie, and she seemed genuinely excited that I would be staying with her. We had met before and had several classes together. As we walked home, she explained that she was the only girl in her family. She had two brothers, one older and one younger. Even though I was feeling awful, just talking to her made me feel better.

As we walked in the front door, I was immediately aware of the mouthwatering smells of home cooking, and they made my stomach grumble. Her home felt warm and welcoming, and after I met the entire family, Stephanie showed me her room where we would both be staying. We quickly settled in and finished our homework, and shortly after, we were called to dinner. Everyone sat around the table discussing the day's events, and before long, I felt totally at ease. The next morning after a pancake breakfast, Stephanie's mother drove us all to school, even though it was only a few blocks away. Although it felt good to be a part of a caring and loving family, I still missed my own terribly and constantly worried about them.

Several weeks passed. My father would call at least once a week to check on me. He told me he was still trying to work things out with my mother, and soon, we would be a family again. When I asked why my mother didn't want me to live with her anymore, he was vague and told me he couldn't answer my question. There was an awkward silence, and with nothing left to say, we hung up. Even though my new foster family was very kind to me, I had to know why my mother no longer wanted me. "Why couldn't she love me?" I wondered. I knew I had to go back home because maybe if I just tried really hard to be a good daughter, my mother would love me and let me live with her again.

Eventually both my father and I moved back home, and we tried to pick up the pieces and be a family. My mother seemed to be living in her own little world and was oblivious most of the time. We all walked on eggshells because of her random outbursts and fits of rage. But perhaps the most difficult time came after her second suicide threat. She was finally placed in the hospital's psychiatric ward for several weeks. When she came back home, she was more withdrawn than ever. She was given some new medication for her moodiness and depression but refused to take it consistently.

The anxiety I had experienced since I was a young child had by this time turned into debilitating panic attacks. As a result, I ended up missing a lot of school. I was spending more time again at my friend Robin's house, which was a safe haven, and her family soon became a second family to me.

I thanked God many times for Robin and her family, as they were often the only bright spot in my life during that time. I used to pretend that I was a part of their family, and I eventually got into the habit of calling Robin's parents, Mom and Dad. No matter what we did, Robin and I never failed to have a good time together. She had a mischievous twinkle in her eye and could always make me laugh. We always had each other's back, and she was the sister I wished I had!

By the time I was fifteen years old, I had had enough of my mother's rejection and cruelty. We had started going to family counseling, and it didn't take long before my mother decided that she wasn't the problem. After the first few sessions, she refused to continue. I was the only one who continued to go, mostly because of my crippling anxiety.

The therapist was very sympathetic and genuinely wanted to help me. We both agreed that I had to get away from my current situation. Moving out seemed to be the only answer. Living with another foster family was completely out of the question for me, so I decided to take matters into my own hands. That summer, while my parents were out of town for the weekend, I was visiting some close friends, and we came up with the idea of moving in together. It seemed to me like the perfect solution!

That weekend, I went back to my parents' house and packed up all my belongings before they returned home. My friend came over with his car and helped me move into an apartment with two other roommates. We all had meager jobs, and between the three of us, we barely managed to keep a roof over our heads. My father was heartbroken when he found out I was gone, but he realized, too, that maybe I was better off this way.

Although my mother had washed her hands of me and couldn't have been happier that I was gone, my father still kept tabs on me. He stopped by to visit without my mother's knowledge and even helped out financially if I needed it. Once my mother found out, she flew into a jealous rage and angrily accused me of being "the other woman." Even though I understood my father felt torn between honoring my mother's unreasonable wishes and still being a part of my life, I was growing tired of being his worst-kept secret!

It was so unfair that my father had to choose between us, and I was always forced to be second best. I was angry and resented him for not standing up to my mother and protecting me, his own daughter. I no longer wanted any part of it, and I grew even more determined to be independent and make it on my own. Even though I was young and scared, I knew I couldn't live this way any longer.

When I turned sixteen, with the help of my therapist, I officially became an emancipated adult! Since I qualified for a special government program for minors, I was able to get a good job in a daycare center, and later on in a school library. It came with benefits and the pay was halfway decent. I was not only gaining valuable job skills but also confidence in my own capabilities. I dropped out of school so I could work full-time, and a year later I earned my G.E.D.

Life was far from easy at that tender age. Sometimes I envied my friends who had such normal lives and loving families to go home to. Most of them had curfews, and I secretly wished I had one, just to feel like someone cared when I got home. How terribly ironic it seemed when my friends said they envied me, and how cool they thought it was that I had my own place! Little did they realize how much it hurt to be so different from them, missing out on all those teenage family memories.

CHAPTER 3

A family of my own

Over the next couple of years, roommates came and went, and I eventually found myself alone. I was somewhat of a wild child by then, hanging out with the wrong people and being rebellious. I decided to seek my fortune elsewhere and move to Tennessee with a friend. It turned out to be an unwise decision. When we got to Memphis, we became lost and found ourselves in the wrong part of town. When we stopped to ask for directions, a menacing-looking thug appeared out of nowhere and stole my car, as well as all my belongings. I considered us lucky, only in the way that we weren't seriously harmed or killed.

Finding ourselves lost and alone on the streets, we walked to a convenience store several blocks away. After explaining what had happened, the clerk called the police. Since we had no money and nowhere else to go, both my friend and I were taken to a runaway house in the heart of downtown Memphis. It was located in a run-down, crime-filled neighborhood.

All the kids there had tragic stories, and were either drug addicts, victims of abuse, or had run away from a dire situation. There were kids of all ages, the youngest being just ten years old. I trusted no one, and always slept with one eye open. The youth counselors did their best to monitor the situations that sometimes happened, but things still managed to get out of hand. It was one of the scariest experiences of my life!

After more than a month had passed, the car thief was caught. We were taken to the police station where we quickly identified him in a line-up behind a two-way mirror. I was lucky enough to get my car back, but little else was recovered. By that time, I had had enough! I decided to call my parents and beg for money to come home. My mother answered the phone, and when I explained where I was and what had happened, she got angry and hung up on me. I had never felt so scared and alone, and I was starting to fear that I was destined for a life on the streets.

The next day, much to my relief, I was told that my father had wired the money. I had never felt so grateful in all my life! I was terrified after my experience, and I couldn't wait to leave this place behind.

After several days on the road, we made it safely back to Bismarck. It was a relief to be back in familiar surroundings, and I temporarily moved in with my friend. I was able to put in a claim on my auto insurance for the stolen items and recover part of my loss.

I eventually settled down and got my life together. I rarely saw my parents, and still felt a lot of anger toward them, resenting them for the life I was forced to live.

I still didn't always make the best decisions, especially when it came to the guys I dated.

One day I was visiting with my friend Karen, and her latest boyfriend, Dave. I had recently ended a stormy relationship with my boyfriend, Jeff, and I was lonely and bored. I decided to invite them over later that evening, and when Karen politely asked if Dave's friend could join us, I quickly agreed.

I was looking forward to having company, and I spent extra time doing my hair and makeup. They arrived right on time, and Karen introduced me to Dave's friend, Randy. He was tall, thin, and good-looking, with brown hair and deep brown eyes. He had a friendly smile and was rather shy.

We had a fun evening, listening to music and playing dice. The next day, Karen suggested that we double date and see a movie together. We all got along well, and I agreed to the date.

Since Randy and I didn't know each other well, and it still felt a little awkward, we decided to all ride together in Dave's car. They planned to pick me up at 7:00 sharp that evening. When the doorbell rang at 6:45, I assumed they had arrived early. I answered the door and was shocked and disappointed to see Jeff standing there, obviously drunk. I quickly told him to leave because I had plans for the evening. He wouldn't take no for an answer and pushed his way inside. He kept trying to apologize and insisted that he wanted to get back together.

A few moments later, I heard Dave's car pull up. I slowly opened the door and invited them in. Jeff was almost passed out in the chair by then, and I couldn't have been more embarrassed. I saw the disappointed look on Randy's face, and I assumed I would never see him again. They left shortly after and went to the movie without me.

Two days later, I was surprised to see Randy coming up the stairs and heading straight to my door. I was carrying some boxes out to the garbage, and he quickly offered to help. He stayed and chatted for a little while and before he left, I agreed to another date. This time, it would be just the two of us. We had dinner together that evening, and later took a long drive talking and listening to music. We started seeing each other regularly after that. Randy was much different from the other guys I dated. He was warm, caring, and affectionate. For the first time, I was starting to feel safe, loved, and protected.

When Randy unexpectedly proposed, I suddenly found myself married at the age of nineteen. I was happy to finally share my life with someone who truly loved me, but all my hopes and dreams of having loving in-laws were not meant to be. I secretly wished that my mother-in-law could have been the mother I always longed for, but my walls were up, and it was difficult for me to let my guard down.

It was rare for Randy and me to argue, but when his parents came to visit things grew tense between us. We found ourselves snapping at each other, and sometimes saying hurtful things. Instead of welcoming me into the family fold, my in-laws made it quite clear that they did not approve of me. They were very strict about their religious beliefs, and I was not the girl they had envisioned for their youngest son. To make matters worse, I didn't belong to a specific denomination. Although I had a strong faith in God, I felt more comfortable being spiritual in my own way, rather than belong to a church.

When they insisted that Randy and I convert to their faith, we stood firm in our decision that we would find our own path to God. Eventually, it became easier for them to blame me for leading their son away from their church, even though it was a decision we both made together before marriage. It soon became a fierce battle with them, putting a strain on our relationship. I understood that I was not destined to be a part of a loving, caring family. I was once again unwanted and unloved. It was yet another painful rejection that I would have to endure.

During our first year as husband and wife, our marriage was constantly put to the test. My mother suddenly wanted to get involved in my life again, mostly due to a lack of anything better to do. Instead of being helpful, she either stopped by unannounced or constantly called to put me down and belittle me. With my mother's harsh criticism and my in-laws' stern lectures, it was almost more than either one of us could take. To make matters worse, I soon discovered I was pregnant with our first child. Although Randy and I were both overjoyed, it added fuel to the fire. Once my in-laws discovered we were having a baby, they became almost unbearable with their crusade. With all the constant preaching and threats of burning in hell, I started to question my own beliefs. I feared that maybe God had rejected me as well.

It was our first Christmas together, and we had planned to spend Christmas Eve at Randy's parents' house, and Christmas day with my parents. On the drive over to my in-laws' house, I suddenly started having contractions. I wasn't due until early January, so we weren't overly concerned. I was feeling very ill-at-ease, knowing how my in-laws felt about me, and I suspected that was the source of my discomfort. By the time we got there, the pains slowly subsided, and I soon felt better. The next day was Christmas, and we were sitting around the dinner table at my parents' house when the pains started again. I noticed they were stronger this time though still irregular. By the following day, I knew that I was in full-blown labor. I called Robin, who lived nearby, and she arrived within minutes. While Randy called the doctor, Robin helped me into the front seat of the car.

On the way to the hospital, I became terrified as the pains grew more intense. I had no one to talk to about having a baby and had no idea what to expect. I was thankful, however, that the two people I trusted most in the world were with me. When we got to the hospital, I was immediately taken to the delivery room. Robin was on one side of me, and Randy on the other. I pushed and screamed, and soon, my son Cory was born. He weighed over eight pounds and looked just like Randy. We were in awe of the miracle we had just witnessed and couldn't have been prouder! Our joy, however, was to be short-lived. By the time we came home from the hospital, Randy's parents had started in on us again, insisting that we have our son baptized in their church. When we refused, they decided to make it their life's mission to break up our marriage. They threatened to have it annulled.

Between my in-laws' threats and my mother's harassment, soon we were at our wits' end. We both knew we would never survive if we stayed where we were. In 1984, a year after we were married, we moved far away from the North Dakota town where we both grew up and set our sights on Colorado. We were both only twenty-one years old and headed for parts unknown. We chased our hopes and dreams, raised our family, and never looked back. It's a funny thing, however, to think you can run away from your troubles. They have a sneaky way of catching up with you and somehow, always seem to find a way back into your life. Looking back, I think that maybe this was God's plan to give my mother and me a second chance before it was too late.

In 1987, our daughter, Carisa, was born. Although Randy was by my side during her birth, I felt even more scared and alone than before. I had a difficult time in the delivery room and lost a lot of blood. My road to recovery was long and painful. We ran a small property maintenance business out of our home, and I managed the administrative duties and took care of sales to keep business coming in. We eventually hired several more employees as business grew. With a newborn and a toddler underfoot, it certainly wasn't easy, but somehow, we managed.

When Carisa turned two, and Cory almost five, I decided to take night classes and earn a degree in medical administration. Although I loved being a mother and felt totally devoted to taking care of my children and helping run the business, it felt good to do something just for myself. I felt lucky to have a husband who fully supported me and never complained about watching the kids in the evening while I was at school. Although there were times when being a mother truly frightened me, I found myself comparing my life to my mother's and often wondered how we could be so different.

We had lived in Colorado for three years but had trouble making friends in a large city that still felt strange to us. Randy's sister and brother, along with their families, lived in the same city, but our relationship with them remained strained due to the obligation they still felt toward my in-laws. Randy and I used to joke that we made such a good couple because we were both the black sheep in our families. It certainly did seem that it was always Randy and me against the world! Even though we didn't have much of a social life, we tried to make time for each other and our children, going to the park or visiting the zoo. But life was still complicated, and far from perfect.

Eventually the lack of close family and friends started to get to me, and I felt lonely and isolated. I was beginning to have serious doubts about myself, not just as a mother but also as a wife. The echoes of the past invaded my thoughts, and I suddenly began to wonder if this is what my mother felt like in the early years of her marriage. It occurred to me that I might follow in her footsteps, and I was suddenly afraid.

When Cory started pre-school in the fall at a neighborhood church, I had hoped to make friends with some of the other parents. While waiting by the door to pick him up, I usually made small talk with other moms and I couldn't help comparing myself to them. They always seemed to have nicer clothes, more interesting lives, and drove better cars. I started to feel strangely inadequate and became less social. Sometimes, I even worried that Randy might find someone prettier, smarter, and better than me. He always reassured me of his love, but I could feel the growing tension between us.

Later that year, the old familiar feelings of fear and anxiety took hold of me as never before. In the past, I was able to struggle through them until I regained my composure. But now, even as I had everything I wanted, it seemed as though my life was spiraling out of control. I developed digestive problems, as well as other health issues. I visited my doctor, but I was afraid to tell him about my anxious feelings for fear of being judged. Nothing seemed to help, and I was growing more miserable by the day.

One day I hit rock bottom, and finally gathered the courage to seek professional therapy. I was determined to work hard and unload the heavy burden I still carried. I knew it was time to make peace with my buried feelings of anger, rejection, and abandonment so I could create a better life for myself and my family.

As the years went on, we put down roots, made new friends, and became more established in our lives. We eventually sold our business, and I got an administrative job at a large hospital, and Randy was hired by another company for a management position.

At least once a year, Randy's parents came to Colorado for a family visit. Because we never actually made peace with them, we kept our distance and sometimes refused to see them all together. It was quite obvious that they had not changed their opinion about me, especially since we were the only ones in the family with a different faith. They would visit Randy's other siblings, convincing them that we were horrible people and that we lived in sin. On the rare occasions that we did see them, it was very tense, and they would scare the kids with their talk of hellfire and damnation.

My parents didn't come to visit nearly as often, but things with them weren't much better. It was always the same scenario: my mother would misbehave and cause a scene, and my father would make excuses for her. As a result, my children were never close to either set of grandparents. I always felt guilty and tried to explain the situation as best I could. I couldn't help but feel that I had let them down because I was incapable of giving them the loving and caring grandparents that they so deserved. I still wrote letters to my grandmother, who was getting up there in age, and I wished my children could know that kind of love. I hoped that someday they would understand, although I didn't even understand it myself. And I had serious doubts that I ever would!

One afternoon, I received a call from my brother, Shawn, asking if he could come and stay with us for a while. He had married less than a year ago, but I wasn't completely surprised when he called since my father had told me earlier that there was already trouble between him and his wife. We had never been what you would call close, but he was my only sibling, and I was happy to help.

A few days later, Shawn arrived with most of his belongings. I made it my duty to take him under my wing while he poured out the whole sad story. After hearing him out, I agreed that filing for a divorce and moving to Colorado was the best solution. I felt sorry for him and couldn't imagine how he must feel after experiencing such a violation of trust so early in their marriage. During Shawn's stay, my mother kept calling and lecturing him about the perils of being a divorced man. She begged him to come to his senses and move back home with them. She even tried to recruit me into taking her side, but I refused to get involved. It became a losing battle, and eventually, she gave up. I couldn't have been more relieved!

Within a few weeks, Shawn was enrolled in university to finish his degree, and I had no trouble helping him find a part-time job. I offered to let him stay with us for as long as he wanted until he got back on his feet again. Shawn soon became a part of our family and even went on vacations with us. The kids enjoyed having him around, and I was glad to have my brother close once more. He was easygoing, much like my father, and we had a lot of catching up to do. It felt good to help out, and I assured him that he was family, and we always took care of our own. I wish that Shawn had remembered those words later on when our parents needed help.

CHAPTER 4

A devasting diagnosis

Ever since we moved to Colorado, my parents would make it a point to call every Friday night. It was my dad's idea of staying in touch. He would call on the downstairs phone extension, and my mother listened on their upstairs phone. The conversation would usually begin with small talk and catching up. It didn't take long before my mother got nasty and said hurtful things to me. She would start monopolizing the conversation and would sometimes even accuse me of being an ungrateful daughter. Needless to say, it would always end abruptly.

Eventually, I just stopped answering the phone on Friday nights. Sometimes she would call several days later and try to apologize for her behavior. She would make random excuses, and inevitably, it turned into the blame game. I always wanted to believe her sincerity when she said she was sorry, and that she would change. But deep down, I knew better. My mother was an angry, miserable person, feeling the need to inflict her pain on others.

It always amazed me how fresh her anger still was over incidents that had happened many years ago, even before I was born. At times she would suddenly become upset and begin carrying on about a childhood argument she had with one of her siblings. Just listening to her rant and rave, you would think these incidents had occurred yesterday! Her desire to live so much in the past was disturbing. As I look back, I know she needed more help than any of us could have imagined.

Early one summer, when my children were both young adolescents, we all went back for a visit to see my parents — something we seldom did. My father had mentioned earlier, in a phone conversation, that my mother was not doing very well. Something about the tone of his voice worried me, so we decided to drive the 700-mile trip to Bismarck. As usual, when we arrived, things were tense, and everyone struggled to be on their best behavior. I couldn't help but notice that the house seemed somewhat untidy, not as meticulous as I was used to seeing. We all sat down in the living room, trying to get comfortable after the journey. When I tried to have a conversation with my mother, she seemed rather distant and had a hard time staying focused.

Since my mother wasn't much for cooking, we decided to have dinner at a nearby restaurant. When the waitress came to take our order, Mom kept getting confused and had trouble communicating what she wanted. After our food arrived, I noticed that her hands shook when she picked up her utensils. She became easily distracted and didn't eat much of her meal. Every time I glanced at my dad he would quickly look away. I could sense that something was very wrong. Over the next several days, I noticed that my mother's behavior continued odd and erratic; she was definitely not acting like herself!

On the day we left to go back home, my dad walked us out to the car to see us off and wave goodbye to the kids. When I asked him about her strange behavior, he admitted that this was something he had noticed over the past several months. He confided how much it was starting to worry him, but wasn't sure if she would agree to see someone. We agreed that something needed to be done soon, so he promised to make a doctor's appointment for her that week and keep me informed.

I got the call from my dad about two weeks later. The doctor felt that my mother's medication for depression should be adjusted; he thought that the dosage was too high. I had a hard time believing this, but Dad seemed to trust the doctor. Even though something in my gut didn't feel right, I told myself the doctor knew his job, and there was no need to worry.

Many of us have complete faith in our doctors and accept what they tell us, even when something doesn't seem quite right. I learned a very important lesson here: if something doesn't feel right to you, it's okay to get a second opinion. Not only is it important, but it could save your life!

Over the next couple of years, my earlier feelings of hurt and resentment had begun to soften, and I kept in touch with my parents through weekly phone calls once again. But every time I heard my mother's voice over the phone, I thought something seemed a little *off*. As time went on, it became my perception of the new normal for my mother.

The following Christmas, my daughter Carisa proudly announced that she and her boyfriend had become engaged. It seemed like only yesterday she was a little girl playing dress-up, and now she had become a beautiful woman. She was still so young, and I marveled at how much like me she was, determined to spread her wings and make her own way in the world. Although we butted heads from time to time, I felt fortunate that we still managed to have a close and loving relationship. Sometimes, I couldn't help comparing her to myself at the same age, and I realized just how far I had come.

Throughout the years, motherhood had presented challenges that brought out my vulnerable inner child, and I would become overly protective. I would find myself getting upset with other adults and teachers and rush to my children's defense whenever I felt they were being treated unfairly or criticized. Especially Cory, who had a slight learning disability when he was quite young.

Life hadn't always been easy, and our family had its share of ups and downs. I realize I wasn't always the easiest person to live with, especially when old familiar doubts and fears nagged at me. There were still those times I struggled with trust and feelings of insecurity. I was always grateful that Randy remained patient with me, and still accepted me for who I was.

We were all excited about my daughter's big day and planned for a mid-summer wedding. The months quickly flew by, and my parents decided to fly out to Colorado to share their granddaughter's special day. They thought it best to stay in a nearby hotel. Since I was very busy,

I suggested that we meet at the church before the wedding for family pictures. It would be the first time I had seen my parents since our last visit, two years earlier.

I had just finished tending to some last-minute details in the bride's dressing room when I decided to look for the photographer. As I came down the hallway, I spotted my parents walking in with Shawn and his new wife. My father looked very handsome in his grey suit and tie, and my mother was very elegant in her pearls and pale blue dress that brought out her eyes. As I got closer to welcome them, I noticed that my mother was stooped over and had a hard time making eye contact. After giving them each a big hug, I told them I would catch up later as I was trying to find the photographer to see about pictures.

Seeing my mother again was never easy, and I felt nervous and on edge. Even though it had been several years since the last big scene, I braced myself for her irrational behavior and harsh words. I still remained cautious and never let my guard down. I had not forgiven her for all the pain she had caused me throughout my life, and I didn't want anything to ruin my daughter's big day.

When it came time to gather at the front of the church for family pictures, I handed out corsages to all the women in the family. My father then politely asked me if I could help my mother with hers. She was struggling as I gently took over the duty of pinning the flowers on her collar. That's when I noticed how badly her hands trembled. When I looked up and saw the drool coming from the side of her mouth, I was shocked! Dad noticed my reaction and discreetly said, "I want to talk with you about it later."

We all managed to get through the family pictures, and the wedding turned out beautifully! The reception was lively, and there were the usual guests to attend to. I worried that my parents seemed ill at ease and kept to themselves. Every time I tried to make my way over to have a conversation with them, I ended up sidetracked by someone or something. I knew I had to find some private time with them before they left the next day.

The following morning the happy couple was off on their honeymoon, and I still had things to clean up and put away. I called my dad and told him I would like to see them both before they left, so we agreed to meet in the lobby of their hotel. When I got there, my mother looked pale and was unusually quiet. My father looked stressed, with more gray hair than I remembered, and I suddenly felt guilty for not seeing them sooner. The conversation consisted mainly of Dad and me talking about their trip and funny things that happened at the wedding. Mom was looking tired by then, and my dad offered to take her back to their room.

He returned downstairs shortly, and we talked more seriously about my mother's condition as he walked me out to the parking lot. He admitted that he was quite worried, and we both agreed it was time for Mom to see a new doctor. We said our goodbyes and I gave him an extra big hug before getting in my car. As I drove back home, I had a sinking feeling in my stomach.

As planned, my father scheduled an appointment for my mother the following week. After doing a thorough examination and running some tests, it didn't take long for this doctor to confirm our worst fears. My mother had Parkinson's disease. We were devastated!

CHAPTER 5

Nebraska bound

Early that fall, my beloved grandmother passed away at the ripe old age of 101. My son Cory and I and my brother Shawn decided to drive back to North Dakota for the funeral. When we arrived, my mother seemed more out of sorts than ever. She was in a foul mood and couldn't seem to understand why we were there. The day of the funeral, my mother said she didn't want to attend the service because she had too much vacuuming to do. I thought it was an odd excuse but decided it was just her way of getting out of the obligation. After all, the funeral was being held in another town almost two hours away.

The next morning everyone, except for my mother, set out to attend my grandmother's funeral. When we returned later that afternoon, I was surprised to see that my mother was still vacuuming. We were gone for at least eight hours! When I asked her how long she had been vacuuming, she said she didn't know and seemed rather confused. I also couldn't help but notice that she was shuffling her feet as she walked into her bedroom, as though walking was a great effort.

Later that evening, I brought out a photo album of my daughter's wedding from the past summer. My mother kept getting everyone in the pictures confused, insisting that they were someone else entirely. She became quite angry when I tried to correct her, so I put the album away. I was tired and didn't feel like arguing. I decided to call it a night.

We headed out early the next morning for the trip back to Colorado. As we talked in the car on the drive back, we all agreed that my mother's condition had progressed. Over the next several months, it was apparent that some drastic changes would have to be made.

By the following spring, it was evident that my father could no longer leave my mother home alone all day. Her behavior was increasingly more erratic. She would occasionally cut up all their credit cards, insisting they were causing them to go into debt. Other times, she would call and harass the utility company, claiming that she had been overcharged. My father would often call me from his office to tell me the latest incident, and I cringed each time I imagined what they must be going through.

My father had recently turned seventy-one and decided it was time to retire. Given the circumstances, he wanted to be closer to family and care for my mother himself. That also meant leaving the state where they had spent most of their lives. Since my brother and I both lived in Colorado, I assumed they would be moving somewhere nearby. But moving to the big city did not appeal to either of my parents, so we decided to look for assisted living homes in surrounding smaller communities. Several places in Colorado may have been worth considering, but the one that held the most interest for both of my parents was a charming place called Crestview. It was only three hours away from Colorado, in a small Nebraska town called Scottsbluff.

Late that May my first grandchild, a beautiful little girl, was born. My parents were very excited to meet their first great-grandchild! They decided to make a trip to Colorado to see the family first, and then on the way back home, stop in Nebraska to visit the assisted living community.

In the meantime, I did my own research on the Internet, and Crestview seemed like a good fit. It had three different care levels, which included skilled nursing. It would allow them to advance to a new level of care as my mother's disease progressed. The grounds were beautiful and even had a duck pond on the front lawn. It was a small enough community where my dad would feel comfortable driving, and there were good medical facilities nearby. We were all in agreement that it seemed like the perfect solution for them. The arrangements were made, and three months later, my parents became proud new residents of Crestview.

As a final act of love and respect, my parents thought it was important to give their late son, Jason, a new headstone for his grave before moving so far away. They both knew that it might be the last time they would be able to visit the cemetery where he was laid to rest so long ago.

Since most of their furniture and other items were either sold or donated, it didn't take long for them to get unpacked and settle into their new home. My parents both agreed it was time to downsize anyway. In just a matter of weeks, they were meeting new friends, enjoying group outings and other fun activities. It appeared that my parents had entered a new phase in their lives. They both seemed much happier and more relaxed than I could ever remember. Each time we came to visit, which happened more frequently now, Dad took great pride in showing us around and introducing us to the other residents. One elderly gentleman had a model train that he worked on as a hobby and proudly put it on display for all to enjoy. Each month he added something new and different to the tiny little make-believe train town, and it soon became the main attraction!

As the months flew by, my parents adjusted well to their new surroundings. They both seemed to like their new doctor and the rest of the medical staff. I was equally impressed when Dad reported how knowledgeable they seemed regarding my mother's condition. On one particular visit, the doctor prescribed some new medication that was thought to slow the progression of Parkinson's disease. A few weeks later, my mother came back for a follow-up visit, and the doctor decided to do further testing. He later confirmed what we had already started to suspect. My mother was diagnosed with early-stage dementia.

According to the National Parkinson Foundation, an estimated 50 to 80 percent of Parkinson's patients will eventually get dementia as their disease progresses. On average, this happens within the first ten years of the onset of Parkinson's disease.

As time went on, I started to notice small changes in my mother's personality. They were subtle at first. It was Easter Sunday, and Randy and I decided to spend the weekend in Scottsbluff visiting my parents. We checked into our hotel room and unpacked our bags, then drove the short distance to their apartment. As we approached the secured building, I felt gratitude once again that my parents had found such a wonderful place to live. I rang the buzzer to their intercom, and a few seconds later, my father answered and said he would be right down. After several moments, he appeared and opened the heavy wooden door to let us into the front lobby. Even though he was smiling, I knew something had happened.

After shaking Randy's hand and giving me a big hug, he seemed to hesitate before leading us up the stairs that led to their apartment. I ask if everything was okay, and he admitted that my mother had fallen at church that morning. She usually held on to Dad's arm for support whenever they went out. She had a walking cane but refused to use it, claiming that she felt more secure holding on to my dad. He explained that when church service let out, she became confused and turned to walk in the opposite direction. Before my dad realized what was happening, she twisted and fell to the ground. His face held so much remorse that my heart ached for him. It was the first time he felt that he had failed to take care of my mother.

Luckily, she only suffered some minor bruising. When I asked her if she was okay, she seemed to have forgotten all about the incident. I had brought with me a beautiful orchid plant and arranged it on a table. When I turned around to ask my mother what she thought, I noticed she was rocking in her rocking chair, completely oblivious to her surroundings. In fact, she was rocking so hard that the chair was starting to move across the room! When I gave my dad a worried look, he simply chuckled and said, "It's become her new obsession." He then admitted that he had a hard time getting her out of the chair to eat or go to bed at night. It was quite obvious that she preferred the constant back and forth movement and was completely immersed in her own little world.

Repetitive behavior is a symptom of progressive dementia, caused by deterioration of the brain that takes away one's ability to make sense of the world. I only wish I knew that then, instead of trying to reason with my mother. Sometimes, I tried convincing her that she would tire herself out, and when that didn't work, I tried coaxing her out of the chair by telling her I had something to show her. No matter how hard I tried, she was beyond comprehension.

As time went on, Dad continued to have faith in their decision to move to Nebraska, and consequently, I did too. That Thanksgiving, I planned to have a large holiday dinner at my home. I was expecting about twenty people, including my parents. As the guests started to arrive, my house seemed to shrink in size very quickly. There were people of all ages, including children, and it was getting rather noisy and chaotic. I had barely sat down when my father announced that my mother had locked herself in the downstairs bathroom. By the time I reached the bathroom, he was in a panic. I kept trying to talk to my mother on the other side of the door, but she wasn't responding. By then, my own panic was growing.

When we finally got the door open, my mother was calmly sitting there, folding a tissue on her lap. We all breathed a sigh of relief! Completely unaware of the commotion she had just caused, she looked up at me and said, "I'm very tired and I want to lie down." I led my mother to the upstairs bedroom and made sure she was comfortable before I went back downstairs again. Dad was waiting for me. He appeared upset and very anxious as he told me that taking care of Mom was becoming more difficult than he had first imagined. For the first time since my parents moved to Nebraska, I began to worry about their future.

CHAPTER 6

The perfect gift

After an uneventful Christmas, we celebrated my father's birthday in early January. Randy and I and Shawn and his wife were all staying in Scottsbluff for the weekend. We went out for dinner at my dad's favorite Mexican restaurant, and then came back to their apartment for birthday cake and opening gifts. Everyone was in high spirits and enjoying each other's company. After we finished cake and coffee, I cleared away the dishes and cleaned up the kitchen while everyone relaxed in the living room. As I looked up, I noticed my mother standing in the doorway of the kitchen. She looked like she was going to start an argument. I just smiled and asked her if Dad was ready to open his gifts. The therapy I had invested in earlier in my adult life had paid off, and I learned to walk away when she was itching for a fight. She continued to glare at me with her arms folded across her chest and didn't say a word. I decided not to take the bait and joined everyone in the living room to watch Dad open his gifts. I didn't want anything to spoil his birthday.

I had gotten my father some house slippers that he had asked for, and some new long-sleeved shirts. Shawn gave him a fancy weather monitor, so my father could see the temperature before going outside. As soon as my father finished opening his gifts, my mother took an interest in Shawn's gift, praising him for how thoughtful and wonderful it was. She looked disdainfully at my gift and said, "Maybe you can do better next time." I was hurt but tried not to take it personally. After all, it was what my father had asked for and said he needed. I had spent many years playing second fiddle to my brother. It was always apparent that my mother favored him, and this was yet another painful reminder. I decided to take the high road and blame it on her condition.

In most people with dementia, personality traits become enhanced and can seem almost magnified. In the middle stages, common personality changes include aggression, agitation, paranoia, and delusions of being threatened. It was yet another important piece of information that I later learned.

Even though I spoke to my parents on the phone every week, I was in no hurry to visit again. Each time I asked Dad how things were going, he assured me that everything was just fine. And of course, I chose to believe him. I had gotten much better over the years about ignoring my mother's tactics whenever she started a fight, but her remarks still hurt, and she always managed to get under my skin, especially when she compared me to my brother.

My mother's birthday fell in March. She had no problem communicating what she wanted me to get her for a gift. She was very specific about the kind of dress she wanted, including the fabric, style, and size. I ordered the exact dress my mother described through the store's online website. I had it gift-wrapped and sent directly to my parents' address.

Later that week, I called to wish Mom a happy birthday and asked if she had received her gift. I immediately recognized the tone in her voice. It was obvious that she was disappointed. To my surprise, she told me that I got it all wrong— the wrong color, the wrong size, and altogether the wrong dress! I had written down everything to my mother's specifications and felt quite confident that I ordered the correct one. Rather than try to argue my point, I simply apologized and offered to get her something else instead. Adding insult to injury, she began boasting about the beautiful bouquet of flowers my brother had sent her. As usual, they were just perfect!

When Mother's Day rolled around, I was still feeling hurt and more than a little discouraged when it came to picking out a gift for my mother. It seemed as though I could never do the right thing, so I procrastinated right up until the very last minute. As I shopped around the store, I found myself in the jewelry section where there was an endless selection of sparkling, shiny things that caught my eye. After giving it much thought, I chose a delicately engraved silver cross necklace that I thought my mother might like. I wrapped it in colorful paper and added a pretty pink bow. I even got a thoughtful Mother's Day card to go with it. That weekend we decided to make the trip to see my parents so that I could give my mother her gift in person.

I held my breath as I handed Mom her gift, and she eyed it suspiciously before deciding to unwrap it. When she finally opened the blue box that contained the cross necklace, her eyes opened wide, and she immediately wanted help putting it on. She stood in front of the mirror admiring the necklace, and by the smile on her face, it looked as though she was pleased. I was surprised and caught off guard when she hugged me and thanked me for the gift. Her shift in attitude made me feel uncomfortable, and I actually squirmed at her sudden display of affection. Even though I was unaccustomed to receiving praise from her, I certainly couldn't deny the sense of pride I felt. It was one small victory for me!

My mother was never a particularly religious person, and sometimes her views on the subject seemed a little distorted. I was surprised to learn later on that this cross necklace became almost an obsession with her. The following week I spoke with my dad on the phone, and he admitted surprise at how much she liked the necklace. The cross symbol became a source of comfort for her whenever she wore it, and she refused to take it off. I couldn't help but feel pleased. There weren't very many things I did that made her happy.

The summer was over before we knew it, and soon, the weather turned chilly, and the trees began losing their leaves. In late October, my father announced that they were going to drive to North Dakota for a family visit. I was surprised and also a little worried, remembering how treacherous the weather could be that time of year. My father was confident that they would be fine and assured me that he would only travel during the daylight hours. He also promised to stay in touch so that I wouldn't worry.

They were going to be gone just a little over a week and had plans to visit both sides of the family. It was also important for my mother to stop by the cemetery to pay their respects and place flowers on Jason's grave. Just two days later, my father called to let me know they had arrived safely at the house of my aunt Ginny, who was my mother's oldest sister. The rest of my mother's side of the family would be coming later that day for dinner, and it was expected to be a joyful reunion. I could hear all the happy voices in the background, and my father seemed excited too. I was glad that they were having a good time, and I was starting to feel a little silly for being so worried.

Over a week had gone by, and I still hadn't heard anything more from my father. I told myself I shouldn't worry, but I couldn't seem to help myself. I turned on the weather channel and searched for the forecast in that area. Sure enough, there was terrible weather headed that way. I quickly calculated the time that my parents would be arriving home and decided to give them a call later that evening. I dialed their number, and I could feel my stomach tighten when it went straight to voice mail.

The next morning, I watched the news again, and this time, the highway that my parents would be traveling on was completely shut down due to poor driving conditions. I was beside myself as I dialed their phone number, praying I would hear my father's voice. There was still no answer. I hung up the phone and felt my pulse quicken. I took a deep breath and rationalized that my dad was quite capable of keeping himself and my mother safe. He would certainly have enough sense to get off the road if the weather turned bad. I said a quick prayer and tried to get on with my day.

Later that evening, the phone rang. Picking it up, I heard my father's voice and felt a wave of relief wash over me. He told me they just returned that afternoon, which was a day later than initially planned. He explained that the weather had turned nasty halfway home, and they took shelter at a cozy hotel in the nearest town. I breathed a sigh of relief as I listened to the rest of his story. I was happy to hear they had a wonderful time on their trip, and I couldn't have been more thankful for their safe return. As I hung up the phone, it occurred to me that our roles had reversed, and I had suddenly become the worried parent!

CHAPTER 7

The love letter

It was hard to believe another year had passed, and Christmas was just around the corner. We decided to visit my parents several days before Christmas so we could exchange gifts and celebrate the holiday with them. We all agreed that it was best to keep things simple. I brought some cold cuts, cheese, and fruit to snack on so we didn't have to go out or cook a big meal.

After we exchanged our gifts, my father asked Randy if he could help fix a problem that he was having with his computer. They both disappeared into the next room, and I was left to entertain my mother. I went into the kitchen to make a fresh pot of coffee and returned a few moments later with a plate of cookies and two steaming mugs. I decided to pull out a box of old family photos from the closet and reminisce about the early days.

With holiday music playing softly in the background, we made ourselves comfortable on the couch near the small Christmas tree with its twinkling lights. We were going through the pictures when I noticed my mother staring at an old faded photo of her and my dad. When I asked about it, she explained that this was their first Christmas together, and commented on how they always had a gift for each other. As I looked up at her, I noticed she had tears in her eyes. When I asked her what was wrong, she covered her face with her hands and began to sob.

I was completely caught off guard and couldn't imagine why she was crying. I wasn't used to seeing this side of my mother, and I must admit that it scared me a little. Once she calmed down, she told me that she felt terrible for not being able to buy my father a Christmas present. She wondered what kind of wife she had become and was sure my dad no longer cared for her. After the words sank in, I was floored! My dad had no problem buying her a gift, as he could easily shop for her on the Internet. But she had no way of giving him a gift in return. Now I was the one who felt terrible! It was something that had never even occurred to me.

With Christmas only days away, it was too late for most of the limited options we had, so I suggested a gift from the heart that she could easily make herself. I offered to help her write a letter to my dad about all the wonderful things she felt for him. She thought it was a good idea, so I found some fancy paper and even some colored pens. She had trouble at first, but I helped her find the right words to say. By the time we finished, it was indeed a beautifully heartfelt love letter to my dad.

When I read it back to her, she was beaming with pride. I told her any man would be very lucky to receive this as a gift from such a wonderful, loving wife. By that time, we both had tears in our eyes. I could see as well as sense her vulnerability, and I was finally able to let my guard down as I visibly began to relax. I believe this was a turning point in our relationship. I was beginning to notice a change in my mother. She was becoming a softer person, more accepting of the world around her. She had more compassion and feeling than I ever realized before.

When Randy and Dad came out of the den, my mother announced that she had a very special gift for my father. My dad looked surprised and glanced first at me, then to my mother. She proudly handed him the envelope that contained her letter. He carefully unfolded the letter and silently read the words. By the time he was halfway through, the emotional impact had become evident, and he choked up. When he finished, he held my mom in a long embrace and whispered in her ear how much he loved her. I could almost feel the love and healing in the room. It was a tender moment between my parents that I will always remember.

When we drove home that evening, I was filled with hope and a new perspective. If ever I felt the true meaning of Christmas, it was now. This was certainly as good as it could get. When I said my usual prayer that night, I asked God to give us all the chance to be the family I always hoped we could be before it was too late.

In the following weeks, I began to feel lighter. The apprehension that had always accompanied me had all but disappeared. My faith was renewed, and I felt a new kind of hope. Even our weekly phone conversations had become much more pleasant, and I found myself looking forward to them.

I was not exactly sure how or when this all happened, but I knew we had entered a different phase in our lives. Whether the change was due to my mother's new state of mind or maybe a shift in the universe, I was okay with it!

We returned the next month to celebrate my father's birthday. I made his favorite chocolate cake, and we hopped in the car once again and headed to Nebraska. When we arrived, everyone was in a good mood, and we visited for quite a while before digging into the cake. Dad seemed pleased with his gifts, and Mom was content, rocking away in her rocking chair as usual.

We all gathered in the living room as I slowly took in the scene before me. I gazed at the family pictures that adorned the walls and bookshelf and quietly observed my parents' aging features. All of a sudden, I was keenly aware of how much time had passed. I realized then that we had become a perfectly imperfect family. My heart filled with love, and I knew I wouldn't want them any other way.

When it was time for us to leave, Mom gave me a big hug and told me how much she loved me, and that she appreciated all that I did for them. She was certainly not the mother I remembered, and it felt as though God had answered my prayer. As happy as I was to hear those words and share this magical day, something deep inside was troubling me. I sensed that I was losing her.

Over the next several days, I couldn't get past the unpleasant feeling that kept gnawing at me. In fact, I couldn't seem to think about anything else! All kinds of thoughts and questions filled my head. I began to worry about the future and what life would be like once my parents were gone. I began to wonder—did we waste too much time? How much time did we have left? I longed for more days like this, and I kept thinking how unfair life could be. Just when you think you have it all figured out, it all changes again. Life could certainly keep you guessing!

CHAPTER 8

The girl with the ponytail

Several weeks had passed since our last visit. One evening I decided to give my parents a call. My dad answered the phone, and his voice was strained. When I asked how he and my mother were doing, I was surprised by his response. Since my mother's speech was now starting to suffer, it was difficult for others to understand what she was trying to say. She had become very self-conscious about this and refused to eat her meals in the public dining area with my father. She claimed that when he spoke with other people at their table, she felt left out of the conversation.

This marked the beginning of their social decline. Even though my father was social by nature, he found it easier to accommodate my mother's wishes and stay in their apartment to eat their daily meals. As the weeks went by, I could hear the growing irritation in my dad's voice whenever I called. It was very out of character for him, and I wasn't sure what to make of it. He later explained that my mother's mobility was getting worse, and it was becoming harder for him to take her out. He also admitted that he felt uncomfortable leaving her home alone for too long because he was afraid, she might try to wander off. It meant that doing necessary errands like getting groceries, picking up prescriptions, and especially, my father's doctor visits, were becoming virtually impossible.

As if that wasn't enough to concern me, he further added that my mother was starting to hallucinate and would sometimes wander around the apartment at night. Her latest episode required my father to get out of bed at 3:00 a.m. and offer ten dollars to an imaginary girl with a ponytail, who was supposedly standing in their kitchen. Somehow my mother's scrambled brain rationalized that if my father gave her some money, she would go away. My poor dad soon learned that it was just easier to play along because there was absolutely no way of trying to reason with my mother at that point.

After listening to all the bizarre details, I had a hard time imagining it but knew my dad was not exaggerating. It was rare for him to ever complain about anything. My first thought was that it was time to advance the level of care to meet my mother's growing needs, and I told him as much. I certainly was not prepared for what my father said next.

He carefully explained that he had spoken to the facility's administrator about my mother's worsening condition and asked about receiving additional care. When my father mentioned that she had dementia, it became an entirely new problem that we had not considered.

Although the facility provided skilled nursing, they were not licensed by the state for cognitive care. It was something we did not anticipate. When my parents had become residents three years earlier, my mother's medical condition only consisted of Parkinson's disease and not dementia.

We were faced with a whole new dilemma! My parents were going to have to move once again. To make matters worse, there was a good possibility that they would be separated for the first time in nearly fifty years. Dad had never bothered to get long-term care insurance. He always felt confident that they would be able to live comfortably on their savings and the generous pensions that he received each month. When we started looking at memory care facilities, we were shocked at how expensive they were, especially without insurance. Medicare only covered a small fraction of the cost. Since Scottsbluff did not have the amenities my mother now required, there was only one option left to consider. My parents would be moving to Colorado.

We began looking for memory care facilities almost immediately. We searched the Internet, and I started making phone calls. I discovered that either there were no openings, or they were much too expensive to consider. It seemed that everywhere I turned there was a problem. Back then, I worked full time in a medical office, and my efforts to help my parents had to take second place to my job. By the time I got home at night, most places were closed, and I was forced to leave a message. I did as much as I could on my lunch breaks, but I still wasn't making much progress.

I decided to ask my brother for help finding a suitable place for our parents. He said he would try, but he was also very busy with his job. In the meantime, my mother was getting much worse. She was having more hallucinations as well as lapses in her memory and judgment. On some days, she would get very angry and not recognize my dad at all. I was getting really worried at this point and knew something would have to be done quickly.

My boss was not very understanding of my situation, so I made the difficult decision to quit my job. Although it meant giving up a paycheck and a life I was familiar with, I felt I had no choice. My parents needed help, and I knew it had to come from me. Even though Randy made a decent living, we would still have to cut back and tighten our belts. We had some money in savings we could fall back on in case of emergency. I assumed my unemployment would only be temporary and planned to look for a new job after my parents were settled.

That following week, there was a terrible snowstorm. I was planning to drive to Nebraska to help my dad, but I had to cancel my trip because of road closures. That afternoon, I got a very strange call.

I could tell it was my dad on the other end of the phone, but he sounded muffled and far away. Suddenly I heard loud yelling in the background and recognized my mother's voice. I couldn't understand what my father was trying to say, but he sounded scared and overwhelmed. When the line went dead, I tried to call back immediately. When no one answered, I went into a sheer panic. I had to force myself to calm down and think rationally. I quickly called the facility administrator and explained to her what was happening. She told me she would go upstairs and check on my parents and then call back. I waited by the phone for what seemed like an eternity.

When she finally did call back, she told me my mother was having some kind of an episode and that my father had been trying to calm her down. A facility nurse came to evaluate her and determined that my mother could no longer stay in their apartment. The decision was then made to take my mother by ambulance to the emergency room. Since my father was not taking this well, she offered to drive him to the hospital herself and stay in touch with me.

After expressing my gratitude, I assured her that I would get there as soon as I could and handle things from there. I called Shawn a few minutes later, to let him know about this latest situation. I begged him to come with me, but he insisted he had too much to do. I was on my own.

Two days later, the storm finally passed, and the roads were cleared. I had spoken with my dad several times over the phone, to stay updated on the latest developments. He explained that my mother had a urinary tract infection, which can exacerbate dementia symptoms and cause distressing behavior. She was still in the hospital, but the local nursing home had agreed to keep her for the next two weeks, giving us more time to find a suitable facility in Colorado.

I packed a bag without knowing how long I would be gone, and the next morning, Randy and I headed to Nebraska. I planned to have my husband drop me off at my parents' apartment, and I would stay with my dad until I could secure a place for my mother. Then, I would drive my parents to Colorado in my father's car. Once my mother was settled in the new facility, I would bring my father home to stay with us for the time being. We all agreed that this seemed like the most logical plan.

When we arrived, Randy carried my bag up the stairs to my parents' apartment and left a short while later to return home. I could see that my poor father was beside himself, and guilt swept over me for not arriving sooner. The hospital was planning to discharge my mother that afternoon, and then we would take her to the nearby nursing home.

When we got to my mother's hospital room, she looked lost and confused. She had a blank look in her eyes as I greeted her, and it was evident that she did not recognize me. She was sitting on the edge of the hospital bed and appeared to be watching something beside her. She kept pointing at the floor and said, "I see a funny little red car driving around the room." Then she looked up at me and asked, "Do you see it too?" Not sure how to respond, I looked at my dad, and he just smiled and shrugged his shoulders. It was apparent the last several days had been tough on him too.

Once my mother was discharged from the hospital, we carefully led her to the car and drove the short distance to the nursing home for her temporary stay. They were expecting us. A nurse led my mother down the hall to get settled in her new room while my father and I went to the administrative office and filled out the necessary paperwork. When we finished, my dad and I went to my mother's room to check on her. When I peeked inside the doorway, I noticed there was a rocking chair in her room. She was happily rocking away and seemed completely unaware of all the changes that were happening around her. For that, I was grateful.

CHAPTER 9

Packing up again

The next two weeks were a blur of phone calls, packing, and making arrangements. At the end of each afternoon, my dad and I would drive over to the nursing home to visit my mother. I always felt welcome when we arrived, and the staff was helpful and friendly. It was an older brick building with bright white trim, and a neatly manicured lawn that sat at the end of a quiet street. The facility was a good size with 160 beds and appeared to be almost full.

When I peeked in her room, she seemed to be content and adapting well, especially since there was a rocking chair to keep her occupied. One day I noticed an elderly woman in the hall harassing another female resident. As I got closer, I watched as she pushed her into the wall. I couldn't believe what I had just seen! Since when did nursing homes have bullies? Call me naïve, but when I thought about nursing homes, I always envisioned sweet old ladies and grandfatherly older men. This was new to me, and I was suddenly very worried about my mother.

The bully gave me a threatening look as I walked past her to my mother's room. My dad was waiting for me, and I was about to tell him what I had witnessed in the hallway. Before I could say a word, this nasty woman was standing in the doorway glaring at us. She looked right at my mother and said, "You don't belong here. Get out!" I quickly got up and told her to leave. With that, I shut the door in her face. I couldn't help but notice the look of surprise when I stood up to her. Apparently, she was used to intimidating people. Dad just chuckled, but I knew I was going to have to tell someone about this if I was going to get any sleep that night!

As it turned out, I didn't get much sleep anyway. The phone rang at about two o'clock the next morning. I had been setting up camp in my father's den and sleeping on the floor because there was no extra bed for me. There was a phone on the desk in the room, but in the pitch darkness and unfamiliar surroundings, it took me a while to answer it. By the time I picked up the phone in the den, Dad had gotten to the phone in the kitchen. We both answered at the same time and heard my mother's voice at the other end of the line.

Imagine our surprise when she told us that she was at a gas station and needed a ride home. Dad and I simultaneously asked frantic questions about where she was and how she had gotten there. Before we could do anything drastic, I heard a gentle voice in the background, asking my mother if she felt better and was ready to go back to bed. She gave a garbled response, and the phone went dead.

The fog finally cleared from my head, and I realized what was going on. I dialed the number to the nursing home, Dad anxiously hovering beside me. It took a while, but someone finally picked up the phone. I quickly explained what had just happened, and she put me through to the nurses' station on Mom's wing. When I spoke to the nurse, she calmly told me that when residents got upset, they often let them talk to their family members because it helped them to calm down. I told her how this had scared my father and me, not realizing that my mother was still at the nursing home, and not at some corner gas station! She apologized and admitted that she should have spoken to us first, before putting my mother on the phone.

The next day Dad and I came for our usual visit. The head nurse caught up with us in the hallway and apologized profusely for the incident the night before. She quickly assured us this would not happen again. Since Mom was only staying temporarily, I decided not to make too much of a fuss. My mother had barely been there a week, and it seemed like there was always some daily occurrence.

I spent a lot of time researching care centers and quickly learned that not all were created equal. Some offered memory care, some did not; others seemed rather restrictive and confining and not all that impressive.

Since I was out of state, and short on time, it would be impossible for my father and me to visit each facility personally. So, I researched them all very carefully. I read reviews, checked safety ratings, staffing ratios, and health inspection reports, as well as cost and insurance coverage.

By the end of that first week, I finally received some good news. I got a call from Elms Village, a memory care facility located not too far from where I lived. I was thrilled when they told me they had an immediate opening. It was a facility that I had researched thoroughly, and it was at the top of my list. I excitedly shared the news with my dad, and we were both very relieved! I secured the room for my mother and made all the arrangements over the phone. We set a date for one week, as we still had more loose ends to tie up before we left Nebraska.

One afternoon Dad and I were packing up some boxes. He suddenly sat down in a nearby chair, with an odd expression on his face. I set my box down and asked him what was wrong. He said he wasn't feeling very well and blamed it on the lunch he had eaten earlier that afternoon. I couldn't help but feel concerned, but he just shrugged it off and continued packing.

The next day we spoke with the administrator at Crestview. I told her we had found a place for my mother in Colorado and would be leaving at the end of the week. I also explained that my father would be staying with me until we could figure out a more permanent solution. She agreed to let us store my parents' furniture and belongings in the apartment until we were ready to have them moved to my father's new residence. He would continue paying the monthly rent until further notice.

I immediately called a local moving company and explained our situation. They agreed to stop by the next day to do a walk through and give us an estimate. The apartment was relatively small, so it didn't take them very long to tally things up. We agreed on a price, put down a deposit, and told them we would be in touch soon. I was starting to feel a glimmer of hope. Things were finally coming together!

By the end of the week, Dad and I were both physically and mentally exhausted. We had once again packed up all my parents' belongings with the exception of some clothing and necessary items they would need when they arrived in Colorado. We also decided to take many of their knick-knacks and various other items to the Good Will store for donation. It was time to downsize yet again. It made me sad to realize that everything was about to change. It was the end of my parents' life together as we knew it. All their trinkets, furniture, and other valued possessions that made their house a home, now seemed insignificant.

The one thing I was happy for was that my mother remained oblivious to the fact that all her precious things that once had so much meaning were now being discarded like yesterday's newspaper. The beautiful ceramic swans my father had given my mother long ago for her birthday, a delicate crystal rose that had been an anniversary gift, and brightly painted bird figurines she collected throughout the years were all wrapped carefully and placed in sturdy boxes. It struck me that the hard truth of the matter is that everything we work so hard for and take such pride in, our homes, cars, and other important things, are only temporary. In the end, they become somebody else's burden.

March first finally arrived—the day we planned to leave Nebraska and start a new chapter in our lives. On that last morning, the sun rose brightly in a clear blue sky as we loaded up my dad's car with most of my parents' clothing and a few other necessities. I packed a warm blanket, a pillow, and some snacks to make sure my mother would be comfortable for the three-hour drive to Colorado.

When we finished packing the car, Dad and I went back inside to say goodbye to some of his friends and neighbors. After receiving well-wishes and shaking hands, we went upstairs for one last look at the place my parents called home for three years. As we stood in the doorway of the apartment for the last time, I was suddenly overwhelmed with emotions. A mixture of relief, sadness, and fear washed over me. I looked over at my father and realized he was probably feeling the same way. I just hugged him and smiled. There just weren't any words to express what we were feeling. We were both lost in our own thoughts, suspended in that moment of time.

When we arrived at the nursing home, I found my mother in the dining area. She was deep in conversation with several other women seated at her table. As I walked across the room, I recognized one of them. The bully had befriended my mother and was now demanding to know who I was. I was flooded with relief when my mother told the woman that I was her daughter. I took this as a good sign that she had recognized me, and I started to feel a little more confident about the long drive ahead of us.

After hugging my mother, I walked down the hall to the nurses' station to collect her medications, medical records, and other necessary paperwork to transfer care to the new nursing home in Colorado. In the meantime, my father took care of financial matters. When it was time to go, I made one last search of my mother's room to make sure we didn't leave anything behind while the nurse helped her in the bathroom. As I was helping her with her coat, my mother insisted that she wanted to stay because she didn't want to leave her friends. I quickly assured her that she had new friends waiting in Colorado, and to my relief, she calmed down. At the mention of Colorado, another woman piped up and said, "I know people there, and I'm coming with you!" She tried to walk out the door with us, but luckily, one of the nurses convinced her to go back inside and finish her breakfast.

I put my mother's small overnight bag in the front seat of the car, and my father sat in the back seat with my mother to help keep her comfortable. After making sure everyone was situated, I got behind the wheel of my father's car and drove towards the interstate. As I was adjusting the rearview mirror, I caught a glimpse of my parents huddled together in the backseat. My dad had his arm protectively around my mother as he held her other hand. They both looked scared and vulnerable. At that moment, I silently vowed that I would do everything in my power to protect them as we headed for the great unknown.

CHAPTER 10

A new beginning

The trip to Colorado went smoothly. We only stopped once along the way so my mother could use the bathroom. When we arrived at Elms Village, I drove right up to the front entrance of the building. It was a larger structure than the one in Nebraska, with maple trees shadowing the grounds, and red flowering bushes that lined the front walkway. A nurse came out to greet us and help guide my mother inside.

Upon entering the front lobby, I noticed that the facility was clean and updated, and immediately sensed a calm atmosphere. As we continued on, I could hear music coming from somewhere down the hall, and I was pleasantly surprised to see that the residents were being happily entertained. It was a big facility with 242 beds and offered a range of services that included skilled nursing and memory care.

It was lunchtime by then, and the nurse found a place for my mother in the dining area while Dad and I went to the administrative office to fill out all the paperwork. When we finished, we stopped by the dining room to check on Mom. As we approached her table, I was thrilled to see that she was settling in nicely. The nurse reported that she had eaten most of her meal and even made a few new friends. So far, so good!

A short time later, we all walked down the hallway to get acquainted with the staff and see my mother's new room. I immediately noticed that her name was already on the door, and her bed was neatly made up with a cozy patchwork quilt. The walls were freshly painted a cheerful shade of peach, and there was a window just beside her bed with a lovely view of the landscaped grounds. She would be sharing a room with another woman named Ellen. There was a pull curtain in the center of the room for privacy. Her roommate was bedridden and slept most of the time, so there wasn't much chance of interaction between the two of them. I was surprised that Mom didn't even seem to notice that there was another person on the other side of the curtain, and never bothered venturing over there.

 I unpacked all my mother's clothes and belongings and neatly arranged them in the closet and small dresser provided for her. I also made a mental list of other things that she would need, such as new socks and undergarments. By the time we finished, my mother looked tired out, and the nurse suggested a nap. Once she was settled, Dad and I toured the facility and got acquainted with the rest of the staff. The first person we met was Nancy, the head nurse, who would be overseeing most of Mom's care. She was a bright, cheerful woman, and I immediately liked her. Next, we met Rachael, the activities director. She had a warm, happy disposition and seemed perfect for her job. Everyone seemed friendly and eager to help. I also took note of the other residents, who seemed well attended and cared for. After taking one more peek at Mom who was still quietly resting, Dad and I decided to continue our journey home.

 When I walked in through the front door of my own house, I couldn't help but feel that I had changed immensely in the two weeks that I was gone. I guess, in a sense, I had. I was now a part of something bigger than all of us. My life had changed so much in such a short period. It was both humbling and frightening. In the blink of an eye, I gave up my income, professional life, and future plans. Now I felt nothing but uncertainty as I floundered in a world that I struggled to understand, and that once again included my parents. I wondered what I had gotten myself into!

 I carried Dad's bags into the front entryway and showed him to his room, where he would be staying indefinitely. As he sat down on the bed, I again noticed a pained look on his face. When I asked him if he was okay, he said he was just tired and could use a nap. I helped him get comfortable and quietly closed the door to his room. I could have probably used a nap myself, but after being gone for two weeks, I had a long list of things that needed my attention.

That evening Randy, Cory, my dad and I all gathered around the table for dinner. I was painfully aware of my mother's absence as I looked at the empty chair beside my father. That's when it hit me. I had to come up with a plan to somehow help keep my parents together. Obviously, my dad couldn't live in the nursing care facility with my mother, but there just might be another way!

I had noticed several apartment buildings and townhomes that were practically right next door to Elms Village. They would be within walking distance for my father, so he could visit my mother whenever he wanted. As I considered this plan further, I suddenly remembered that Cory had been talking about moving out on his own but couldn't afford to do so without a roommate. Cory was a kind, gentle soul who lived life at his own pace. He had recently turned twenty-five and was eager to live on his own for the first time. He worked full-time at a car dealership, and I knew he was responsible and hardworking. I was starting to believe I had the perfect solution!

I planned to find an apartment to rent located near Elms Village. It would preferably have two bedrooms and two bathrooms, so my dad and Cory could each have their privacy yet share a common living area and kitchen. The two of them had always been close and shared a good relationship. My son was in his mid-twenties, and I was worried about the age difference, but neither one seemed to have a problem with it. Cory was anxious to help his grandfather during this time, and knowing that my father wouldn't be living alone was a huge relief to us both. When I discussed my idea that evening at dinner, everyone was in agreement, so we decided to start looking at apartments the very next day.

As luck would have it, there was a vacancy in one of the apartment complexes located just behind Elms Village. It was exactly what we had hoped to find. It was spacious with two bedrooms, two bathrooms, and on the ground floor so Dad didn't have to worry about stairs. It was perfect! That very afternoon, my dad and Cory signed a one-year lease and made plans to move by the middle of the month, which was only two weeks away.

That evening I called Shawn and gave him an update on all the recent events. He agreed that it all seemed like a good idea until I asked for his help with moving Dad into the new apartment. I told him that I had contacted the movers in Nebraska, and they would be bringing all our parents' furniture and belongings in two weeks. All he would have to do is help unpack boxes and get things set up. After a brief silence, he told me that he and his wife were planning a trip during that time and wasn't sure if he would be available to help. He also added that he was planning to visit our mother that weekend and check out the new facility. Before we hung up, we finally agreed to touch base at the end of the week to discuss things further.

The following week I received an email message from Shawn informing me that he had indeed visited our mother at the new facility. I could hardly believe my eyes when I clicked on the message. It read, *"Is this really the best you could do?"* I was shocked! After all, I had only two weeks to find and arrange a suitable place for our mother. I had spent hours and days doing research and making phone calls. I even quit my job to accomplish all of this. On top of all that, I had our father to think about as well. It is impossible to describe how angry I felt at that moment. He could never be specific about what he didn't like about the facility. It seemed to me that it was just easier for him to be disagreeable.

Because he had made no mention in his email about helping us move, I decided to give my brother a call. When I mentioned it again, he reluctantly agreed to come by for part of the day to help, since his wife had other plans. I figured it was better than nothing, so I gave him the address and time to meet us there. Even though I was still hurt and angry about his email, I decided to broach the subject of my mother's care facility in person, at a more appropriate time. The last thing I needed was a family argument on my hands to add to my stress.

The next day, I had grocery shopping to do, and Dad wanted to tag along. As I was putting the bags of groceries into the trunk of my car, he walked around to the passenger side door and said that he would sit in the car and wait. On the drive home, I noticed he did not look well, and when I mentioned it, he said he thought he might be coming down with something. When we got home, I suggested that he relax on the couch while I put the groceries away, and then I would fix him something to eat. I had almost finished putting things away when I noticed him standing in the doorway of the kitchen with an odd expression on his face. When I asked him what was wrong, he said he had a funny feeling in his chest that felt like a pulled muscle. Panic rose in my stomach.

Since my father has a history of heart problems, I considered this an emergency. Despite his arguments, I drove him straight to the emergency room. When we arrived, they immediately took him to an exam room where they started doing tests. The doctor later confirmed that he had not had a heart attack, but he suspected a blockage in one of his arteries. He thought it was best to keep my father overnight for observation, just in case.

After they took my father up to his hospital room, I decided to call Shawn and tell him what had happened. I was still feeling quite worried, and I begged him to come to the hospital. Since he lived only fifteen minutes away, he agreed to come. He typically worked from home and said he just had to make a quick phone call to his supervisor before he left.

A few moments later, I went back to Dad's hospital room to check on him. When I walked in, I was relieved to see him smiling; he seemed more comfortable now. When I told him that Shawn was on his way, he seemed pleased that my brother was coming. As we waited, my mind raced ahead, and I realized that I would have to find a local doctor and heart specialist for my father immediately. The attending doctor had given us a referral to see a specialist, so I asked for a list of family physicians in our area as well. It seemed as though my to-do list was never ending.

As soon as Shawn walked in, I noticed he seemed irritated by the idea that he was expected to come. I patiently explained that Dad had not had a heart attack, but a blockage was suspected, and the doctor felt it was necessary to keep him overnight for observation. After listening to my brief report, he pulled up a chair and visited for a short while before announcing that he must get back to work. I thought it was odd since he had mentioned earlier that his supervisor understood that our father was in the hospital, so I asked why he had to leave so soon. Shawn seemed almost defensive as he stood to leave and grumbled something about having a lot of work to do.

After he left, I tried to smile and put on a happy face for my dad's sake. But deep inside, I was seething! I was frustrated and angry by all my brother's excuses to remain absent during the most critical times, not to mention his lack of help and support. I couldn't figure out why he was acting like this. Was this just his reaction to stress? Maybe keeping his distance was just a coping mechanism he used to deal with all our parents' sudden changes. When things settled down, I planned on having a sibling-to-sibling talk about sharing the responsibilities of our parents' care. It was becoming harder for me to deal with this alone, and I needed some help.

I was beginning to worry about my future and our financial situation. How long could I be unemployed before we felt the strain? How would it affect my retirement? At some point, I hoped to pick up where I left off and find a new job in another medical office. I was beginning to miss my professional life, my colleagues, and the usual office camaraderie. If only things were that simple!

CHAPTER 11

Learning about Lewy

The next morning, I brought my father home from the hospital. I already had an appointment scheduled with a cardiologist for the following day, but I continued to keep a close eye on him. He seemed more tired than usual, so I suggested that he lie down and rest when we got home.

The next day, his cardiologist ran several tests and agreed that there was an obstruction in his artery. We scheduled a procedure called a coronary angioplasty for the end of the week. It would involve inserting a stent into his coronary artery to restore proper blood flow to the heart. The doctor admitted that he would not know what percentage of his artery was blocked until he performed the actual procedure.

Three days later, we were back at the hospital for Dad's procedure. I squeezed my father's hand and kissed his forehead before they wheeled him down the hallway into the surgical area. As I headed towards the waiting room, I felt more alone than ever. There was no one I felt like calling. Most of my friends and ex-coworkers had no idea what was happening in my life and had moved on without me. My brother opted not to come, which didn't surprise me, so I told him that I would call as soon as Dad was out of surgery.

I tried to concentrate on the book I was reading, but my mind raced as thoughts of recent events filled my head. Both of my parents were now living in Colorado; my mother was in a nursing home with Parkinson's dementia, and Dad had a whole list of health problems. I was starting to get a glimpse of how things were going to be. Both of my parents needed help, and their list of issues kept getting longer and longer. "Where was it going to end?" I wondered. I was beginning to feel completely overwhelmed!

When the doctor finally came out of surgery, he sat down to talk with me about my father's condition. He said my dad had a ninety-five percent blockage of his coronary artery, and a stent had been successfully placed to keep the artery open. He also mentioned how lucky my father was that they had gotten to him in time. If he had waited much longer to have this procedure, the outcome could have been very different. I shuddered to think about what might have happened if both my parents were still living in Nebraska. I was starting to believe that we had angels watching over us!

I took Dad home the next day. I already noticed an improvement. His color was much better, and he seemed to be in good spirits. He also had a new list of medications that we had to monitor. The doctor instructed him to take it easy for the next several days. In a week, he was expected to resume his normal activities. Because of my father's growing health issues, and the fact that he was obviously not comfortable driving in the city, he voluntarily handed over his car keys. We both thought that it was for the best, and I was relieved. It was one less thing I had to worry about.

The next two weeks flew by. Between keeping track of my mother's progress at the nursing home and taking my dad to his many doctor appointments, I was exhausted by the end of the day. I still had to send for my parents' medical records from their previous doctors in two different states so that we could continue their medical care here in Colorado. At the same time, I was also learning how to become a legal representative and power of attorney for both of my parents. There was so much to learn about this new role I had suddenly acquired. I was now officially my parents' caregiver and advocate!

A few days after my father's procedure, we went to visit my mother at the nursing home. I tried my best to explain about Dad's procedure and reassured her that he would be okay now. She just nodded her head and smiled, then asked where my brother was. I explained that he was working and would probably visit soon. That seemed to make her happy for the moment. Just then, I noticed Nancy, the head nurse, walking down the hallway. I wanted to catch up on my mom's progress since I had been so busy with my dad lately. I left him to visit with my mother while I caught up with Nancy.

She told me that she had meant to call me to discuss some things about my mother. She said her balance was getting much worse, and they would like to start doing physical therapy twice a week. They also planned to do a speech evaluation as well as some further cognitive testing. I thought it was a good idea and told her that I would talk to my father about it. On my way back to Mom's room, I could hear my parents having some sort of discussion. Dad kept explaining that he couldn't live there with her. When I asked my mother what was upsetting her, she got angry and said, "Your father just left me here all alone!" She was obviously having a hard time understanding why Dad couldn't move in with her.

I immediately noticed the devastated look on my dad's face. I tried my best to explain to my mother that my dad would be living very close by and would visit her every day, and she finally started to calm down. The aide peeked her head in the doorway and announced that it was time for lunch. Dad and I both gave Mom a big hug and said that we would be back the next day. As Dad and I left the building, I was feeling even more confident about my plan to have my dad living nearby. It seemed to be the only logical way to keep them together.

A few days later, I received a phone call from my mother's doctor to discuss the results of her medical tests. She started by telling me that while my mother's condition had obviously progressed, the real concern was her actual diagnoses. The cognitive tests showed that my mother's Parkinson's disease dementia was believed to be Lewy body dementia (LBD). It was something I had never even heard of before. The doctor quickly explained that this type of dementia was much more progressive and could also cause hallucinations and severe psychiatric symptoms. In fact, LBD is the second most common dementia after Alzheimer's. In the broad scheme of things, this was yet one more issue we would have to address.

After explaining all of this to my dad, we decided to do some of our own research on the subject. It raised some very interesting questions. How long had my mother had this kind of dementia? Could this possibly explain some of her much earlier behavior? Since there is still very little information known about this disease, we could only speculate that it was certainly a good possibility.

The following week was my mother's seventy-first birthday, so I planned a party at Elms Village and invited the whole family. I reserved one of the large rooms they provided for meetings and special occasions and ordered refreshments from the facility's kitchen. I decided my mother was going to be queen for a day! I manicured her nails, fixed her hair, got fresh flowers, and baked her favorite cake with caramel icing. Everyone arrived later that afternoon for the birthday celebration. After everything was settled, I went down the hallway to get the guest of honor. I told my mother we had a party to attend and she seemed very excited. She had on her favorite blue outfit and looked very pretty. When we walked into the party room, everyone wished her a happy birthday. She seemed a little confused but was in awe of all the balloons, flowers, and decorations.

She kept asking whose party this was, and I reminded her again that it was her birthday. She just nodded and smiled as I handed her another present to open. When it was time for the birthday cake, I lit the candles, and we all sang "Happy Birthday." As we waited for her to blow out the candles, she just stared at the cake, unsure of what to do. Dad came to the rescue and blew them all out for her. Everyone clapped and wished her well. As I was serving the cake, I noticed her head was starting to droop, and she looked tired out from all the festivities. We took a few more pictures, and then I took her back to her room so that she could get a nap in before dinner.

After the party decorations were taken down and the room cleaned, I was exhausted but thankful that the day had gone so well. Even if my mother had trouble remembering that it was her birthday, she could still feel the love we all had for her and each other. I realize that it is in times such as this that we learn to appreciate the moment and just be, no matter what the circumstances. When I look back as I write this, one of the most important lessons I have learned from this journey is gratitude. Just when I think there is nothing left but life's problems, being grateful for the smallest of gifts puts things into perspective.

Before falling asleep that night, I said my usual prayer and gave thanks for all the blessings that had been bestowed upon us. There was peace in our world tonight, and I couldn't ask for any more than that!

CHAPTER 12

The odd couple

The day finally came for my dad and Cory to begin a new life as roommates! I felt relief just knowing that my dad wouldn't have to live alone, and he would still be able to see my mother as often as he liked. I was equally glad that my son had such a good roommate to share his first apartment! We jokingly referred to them as *The Odd Couple*, in reference to the 1970s TV comedy series.

The movers arrived at the apartment on time, and as promised, Shawn arrived shortly after. We all got to work unpacking boxes and getting things set up and put away. Finally, at the end of the day, it started to look like home. It was getting late, and my father suggested dinner at a nearby restaurant. We were all exhausted, and he insisted on treating us for our hard work and efforts.

When I got home that evening, the house felt different. I realized that not only was I now an empty nester because my last child was gone, but it also felt strange not to have my father under the same roof. We had been through so much together lately that I was getting used to his constant presence. As I observed the empty room that once belonged to my son, I again felt a shift that reminded me of how profoundly my life had been affected over the past several months.

I was beginning to miss my old life and routine. My friends and former co-workers rarely called anymore. I no longer had free time to spend with them, and we had nothing left in common. In the beginning, my friends told me how lucky I was that I could give up my job and care for my parents. Somehow, I don't think luck had anything to do with it. I was no longer free to come and go as I pleased. I now had other obligations, and I accepted it. My job wasn't over at the end of the day;

I was on call 24/7. I was stressed and worried, and I couldn't remember the last time I felt relaxed.

I had identified so closely with my job over the years that it felt strange and frightening to be without an income or a workplace at the age of forty-five. I felt like a face without a name. I could no longer recognize myself, and I was beginning to feel disconnected as never before. One day out of desperation, I did a Google search and found several online support groups for people who cared for their parents. I was shocked to see so many others in the same situation and soon learned there was a growing population of people known as "caregivers."

The next morning, I called my father to see how he was adjusting to his new living arrangement. He seemed pleased with the new setup and said he planned to walk over to the nursing home after lunch to visit Mom. He told me he would call when he got home and give me a full report. I sensed a new kind of dedication in my father. Now that he was no longer solely responsible for my mother's care, he was much calmer and more relaxed. He could finally focus on maintaining his relationship with my mother throughout her illness.

One beautiful spring day, my father and I decided to take Mom outside in her wheelchair for a stroll through the flower gardens. Almost as soon as we got outside the door, I noticed that she was becoming agitated. As we walked along, I commented on the warm weather and picked a daisy for her to enjoy. When I handed her the flower, she became more agitated and said she was lost. I tried to reassure her, but then she started yelling and suddenly shrieked, "I want to go back home!" Not knowing what else to do, I quickly turned around and took her back inside, hoping that she would calm down. By the time we got back to Mom's wing, her voice was even louder and echoed down the hallway. A nurse quickly came running over to see what all the commotion was about. By then, she was having a full-blown meltdown.

When we got back to her room, she had calmed down a bit. I told her I was sorry, and we would stay inside from now on. The look in her eyes told me she had no clue what had just happened. I hugged her and sat with her until she became sleepy. A few minutes later, the nurse came in and helped us put her to bed for an afternoon nap. Dad and I left, feeling drained. Lately, she seemed to be having more bad days than good ones. Or so it seemed!

The next day, I got a phone call from Nancy. I was expecting to hear more bad news, but instead, she told me that Mom was having a very good day. In fact, my mother was asking to see me, and Nancy suggested that I come for a visit. I agreed to stop by that afternoon. As soon as I walked through the door, my mother's eyes lit up as she held out her arms to hug me. I sat down with her, and we talked for what seemed like hours. I filled her in about all that had been going on with everyone in the family, and she seemed surprised and shocked as she took it all in. What seemed to surprise her most was when I told her that she was now living in Colorado, and Dad was living in an apartment just one block away. I was amazed that she seemed to understand everything I told her, including the fact that she had Parkinson's dementia. It was as though she had awakened from a very deep sleep!

It almost reminded me of old times, only better because I didn't have to walk on eggshells, fearing that she might become offended and start an argument. She was like a completely different person! After I left Elms Village, I stopped by my dad's apartment and told him about it. He was also very surprised, especially considering her outburst in the garden the day before.

When I got home, I couldn't wait to share my experience with all my friends in my caregiver support group. They had become my lifeline, and I tried to make it a point to check in daily. Many of them admitted to having similar experiences. They explained that although it feels like a wonderful breakthrough, it is only temporary. It usually only lasts for a few days or even a few hours. They also warned me about the mental letdown one feels when everything goes back to the way it was. My friend, Linda, who had cared for both her parents for over a decade, shared that it was a devastating experience, for both her and her father.

With that in mind, Dad and I decided to visit her again the next day. To our surprise, she was still very alert and coherent. My mother welcomed us both as we entered her room and told us she was glad we came. She even remembered details from our conversation the day before, including where Dad lived. After several more days of total clarity, we were all starting to wonder if someone had made a mistake and she didn't really have this terrible disease after all. I found myself looking forward to visiting her. For the first time in my life, I started to feel a close bond. I suddenly felt as though all my prayers had been answered, and I finally had the mother I always wanted! I was starting to believe in miracles and felt great anticipation each time I visited. It was as though I had been given a wonderful gift. I prayed for more days like this before the magic disappeared.

But before we knew it, the spell was broken. By the following week, the nurse called to tell me that my mother was disoriented and not eating well again. I stopped by for a visit that afternoon and noticed right away that the familiar vacant look in her eyes had returned. I tried to remind her of our recent conversations and the time we had just spent together. But she had no recollection whatsoever.

I was heartbroken and longed to have my mother back. I felt rejected and alone as painful childhood memories invaded my thoughts. Frustrated and anxious, I thought that if she only tried hard enough, or if I could just find the right words to say, she would come back again. But each time I tried, it seemed to make matters worse. I remembered my friends' warnings. Now I knew exactly what they meant!

Early the next morning at 3:00 a.m., I awoke to the sound of my phone ringing. Fearing the worst, I quickly grabbed the phone sitting next to my bed. The nurse told me that my mother had gotten out of her bed, fallen and hit her head on the nightstand. Other than a nasty bruise and a lump on her head, she seemed to be doing fine. But just to be sure, a doctor would come and check her first thing in the morning.

It was quickly becoming a nightly occurrence. Every night she would get out of bed and wander around her room and become agitated. The nurses tried to keep an eye on her, but there was only so much they could do. We decided to try a floor alarm that would make a loud beeping sound as soon as her feet touched the floor. It alerted staff whenever she got out of bed, but it didn't really solve the problem.

Next, we installed a special mattress that was somewhat sunken in the middle and had raised sides, making it more difficult for her to get out of bed. That seemed to do the trick, except for her loud protests. As her behavior became more erratic, she would yell and curse at the staff, sometimes even taking a swing at them. I knew she was becoming quite a handful, and I felt terrible for the staff members who cared for her. Each time they told me about one of her incidents, I always felt inclined to apologize on her behalf. It gave me a whole new appreciation for what these people have to endure!

As things got worse, one of the doctors suggested running some tests. To our surprise, my mother had a very nasty urinary tract infection once again. It was what was believed to be causing her violent outbursts. Once the antibiotics took effect, things started to calm down. Much to everyone's relief!

It is surprising to realize that something as common as a urinary tract infection can affect people so differently. It often causes sudden confusion and distressing behavior in older adults and people with dementia, especially women. When younger people get a urinary tract infection, they usually experience the typical symptoms, which are painful burning urination, lower back pain, fever and chills. But symptoms in older adults can be different, mainly because of how their immune system responds to the infection. A UTI is usually caused by bacteria that moves upward, infecting the bladder and kidneys. The infection eventually travels to the brain, where it causes delirium. Since this was something my mother frequently struggled with, I did a lot of research to further understand these effects. However, the reason for the connection between UTI's and sudden behavior change is still unknown.

One afternoon, I walked into her room and was surprised to see my mother taking all her clothes out of the dresser. She looked up at me and smiled as she continued to fold each piece neatly and place them on her bed. When I asked what she was doing, she excitedly told me that she was going on a trip. She then asked if I knew where her suitcase was and if I would get it for her. I decided to play along and asked where she was going. She said she had big plans and was moving to a new town where she could open her own beauty salon.

I suddenly remembered when I was young that my mother always talked about pursuing her profession as a beautician. But instead, she stayed home to be a wife and mother. I realized then that I never even considered the fact that my mother once had hopes and dreams of her own.

As I watched her plan for a future that would never be, I knew deep down that this was something my mother had always wanted. I started to see her in a new light as I imagined her as a young woman, struggling to find her purpose in this world outside of being a wife and mother. Instead, she buried that dream and did what she thought was expected of her. I was starting to get a glimpse of who she was as a person, and not just my mother.

CHAPTER 13

Rock around the clock

Mother's Day arrived, and I decided to bring my mother a beautiful silk flower arrangement for her room. As I was arranging them on her dresser, she happened to notice the vanilla coffee latte I had brought with me. She seemed intrigued and asked, "What is in that pretty cup?" I told her what it was and asked if she would like to try some. She nodded yes, so I went down the hall to find a small paper cup for her. I ended up sharing most of my coffee latte with her, and from then on, it became our special treat!

While I was visiting with my mother that afternoon, I noticed that she had a new neighbor across the hall. She was a stylish woman adorned with bold costume jewelry and had curly brown hair. This woman certainly had no trouble getting around, and the nurses warned me that she liked to wander into the other residents' rooms. Several days later, I noticed that both my mother's desk calendar and the silk flowers I had gotten her for Mother's Day were gone. Following a hunch, I walked across the hallway and peeked into the new neighbor's room. Sure enough, they were both there. After returning both items to my mother's room, I decided to mention it to the staff.

Nancy told me that this was a habit of hers and advised me to take home anything that I thought was valuable or breakable. I wasn't happy about it, but I understood the problem. When I returned, I noticed the woman was in my mother's room again, and they were having quite a conversation! I stayed by the doorway to listen, mainly so I could determine if this woman was on friendly terms with Mom.

I was pleasantly surprised at what I heard. My mother and her new neighbor were chatting away like old friends. They discussed everything from what was on television to what they had for breakfast. I also noticed that Mom was happily sharing her coffee latte with her new friend. I later learned that the woman's name was Ruth, and she also had dementia.

From then on, my mother had a new friend. Every day Ruth would join my mother in the dining room for meals, and they would do activities together. My only concern was when my mother's glasses and slippers started to disappear. Once again, I alerted the staff and let them know that Ruth was now wearing my mother's glasses, as well as her slippers. Rachael, the activities director, was particularly watchful, and everyone tried their best to monitor the situation. But it was almost impossible to prevent since they spent so much time together. At least I always knew where to find the items.

One afternoon as I was walking down the hallway looking for my mother, I overheard some oldies music coming from the dining area. When I spotted her, I was absolutely stunned as I watched my mother clapping her hands and swaying back and forth to the popular song, "Rock Around the Clock." She seemed so uninhibited, without a care in the world. I had never in my life witnessed that part of her, and I couldn't help but wonder what she was like before she became a wife and mother. I was really seeing a whole new side of my mother lately. Without all the emotional constraints holding her back, a different person was beginning to emerge. The dementia made it possible for my mother to "forget" all the things that prevented her from being happy in the first place. I just stood there for what seemed like hours, watching my mother having the time of her life. I will always cherish this memory of her, happy and free of her burdens at last, even if it only lasted for one afternoon.

Ever since my father moved into his new apartment, he made a daily routine of walking over to the nursing home to visit my mother, and when he returned home, he would call and share the details of their visits with me. On this particular day, however, my father told me that there had been an incident. My mother was insisting that he give her the car keys so that she could go shopping. In fact, she was so upset that the nurse had to be called in. Not knowing what to do, my father just left and walked back home. We both assumed she was just having a bad day and would eventually forget the whole thing.

By the next week, it was clear that my mother was not going to let this one go. She wanted her keys, and she wanted them now! My father found some old keys that he had lying around, along with a colorful plastic key chain. The next time he went to visit her, as usual, she started arguing with him about the car keys. He pulled the set of keys out of his pocket and dutifully handed them over. It seemed to satisfy her, and she quickly stashed them in the pocket of her sweater and insisted on keeping them with her. The nurses were aware of my mother's fixation with her keys, and they had a tough time getting her to put them away at night or during bathing. Even her friend, Ruth, didn't stand a chance of getting those keys away from her!

The following week was my parent's forty-ninth wedding anniversary. My father wanted to do something special, so he bought some non-alcoholic sparkling champagne, plastic champagne glasses, and flowers. He also had a tape recorder with some soft romantic music to set the mood. We shared my father's plans with the nursing staff and told them about their special day. The nurses were pleased and commented on how romantic they thought it was. They decided to help my father with his plan by calling him at home as soon as my mother was awake from her afternoon nap. We were all hoping that she would be in a pleasant mood after she was well-rested.

The next day was my parents' anniversary. The staff did their part to make sure everything went according to plan. As soon as my mother woke up from her nap, the nurse called my father, and he walked the short distance to the nursing home with his gifts. The nurse even went out of her way to make sure my mother looked nice for her special day. She put her hair up in a bun and placed a flower in it.

When my father got to her room, he wished his wife a happy anniversary and kissed her on the cheek. He presented her with flowers, poured her a glass of mock champagne, and turned on some soft music.

When he sat down next to her and started to give a toast in celebration, my mother suddenly set her glass down and flatly announced that she already had a boyfriend. When my father tried to remind her that he was her husband of forty-nine years, she became very defensive and said, "I can't possibly expect you to always take care of me." She further explained that she felt sure her new boyfriend would propose marriage any day now and even offered to show his picture. My father was heartbroken. When he walked out of her room a short time later, the nurses all noticed the devastated look on his face.

That afternoon, I was happily anticipating my father's call to hear all about their romantic rendezvous. But as I listened to his story, my heart ached for him. I knew how much he was looking forward to this day, and no one could have imagined the outcome.

My mother was changing drastically before our very eyes, and it was becoming harder to recognize the person we both knew and loved. As dementia progresses, fluctuating personality and behavior changes are quite common. It is usually during this time that family members often choose to seek out support groups, to help them understand these changes. Even though Dad and I were given plenty of material and pamphlets for these kinds of groups, we decided to support each other instead. One of the most difficult things in the world is to mourn the loss of somebody who is still standing right there in front of you. I believe the grieving process starts when these changes begin, and you are no longer able to find the person you miss so badly. For those who have ever loved or cared for someone with a cognitive disease, this kind of loss is devastating.

CHAPTER 14

Strike three!

As summer came to an end, the changes in my mother became more striking. I never knew what to expect. One afternoon, my mother's physical therapy aide caught up with me. She gently informed me that my mother seemed very confused lately. She explained that each time she came to my mother's room to take her down the hall for her exercises, my mother thought that she was her daughter, and called her by my name. We both had blonde hair, but the resemblance ended there. One day she told everyone in the exercise room how proud of her daughter she was! I thanked her for letting me know but wasn't quite sure what to think of it.

When I got to my mother's room, it was quite apparent that she didn't recognize me. With a serious expression on her face, she politely asked, "Could you possibly help me study for a test?" She carefully explained that she had been much too busy lately and couldn't seem to find the time to study.

Not at all sure where this conversation was leading, I decided to take a cautious approach. I asked my mother what she was doing with her time lately and why she was so busy. She seemed almost shy when she replied, "It's because you give me too much homework." I was a little perplexed, but as usual, I just played along and reassured her that I would keep that in mind the next time and she visibly relaxed.

The rest of our visit felt odd and a bit uncomfortable. It was a whole new concept for me, one I wasn't sure I was ready for. Especially when I had to pretend to be someone else other than her daughter. Once again, I felt my mother slipping further away. I was overcome by a deep sadness when I realized that my identity had been erased from my mother's memory. But that was soon replaced by a gnawing sense of fear as I began to feel the weight of her dementia.

I left feeling baffled, not sure what to make of this new phase. I stopped by my dad's apartment before going back home and told him about it. He explained that so far, she had recognized him and that hopefully, this would just be a passing thing with her.

I felt a little better after talking to my father about it. Probably she would remember me again soon. After all, I was her daughter. I was having a hard time wrapping my head around this whole idea. How could someone's memory be erased, just like that? I couldn't imagine not being able to recognize my own children, husband, or grandchildren. I began to worry that I myself could suffer Parkinson's dementia one day, as some cases are genetic. I even began to wonder what would happen if my father got dementia or even my own husband. It was a frightening realization! Dementia is a cruel disease that really does affect everyone, including—or perhaps especially—family and loved ones.

I began mentally preparing myself each time I visited my mother. It was starting to take an emotional toll on me, especially when she became unpleasant. I found myself not wanting to visit her as often as I did in the beginning. Even my dad was now having a hard time with her. One day she could be very receptive and pleasant, and on other days she would become nasty and say ugly things. I never knew who I would be visiting, Dr. Jekyll or Mr. Hyde! Even though I had spent a lifetime being subjected to her unpleasant behavior, this was much different, mostly in the way of how randomly it appeared, and how seldom it made any sense. We all knew it was just the disease talking, but sometimes it was hard to take.

The funny thing about all of this was that she would always ask about my brother and would long for his company. I always told her the same thing, "Shawn is busy, and he will visit soon." Whenever I mentioned his wife and daughter, she seemed shocked that he was married and had a child. It became routine with her, and I just accepted it. My brother did visit on occasion, usually on the weekends, but she could never seem to remember.

Before we knew it, the holidays were approaching. Elms Village took on a festive atmosphere, as the staff prepared for the Thanksgiving holiday. It would be my parents' first major holiday spent apart. Although there was a turkey dinner that they offered to the residents and their families, we decided to visit her the day before the holiday instead.

The next day was Thanksgiving, and the whole family arrived at my house for the holiday dinner. As I looked around the table, I thought back to the previous Thanksgiving when we were all together. I couldn't help but feel a twinge of pain as I observed my mother's absence once again. I knew my father was thinking the same thing as our eyes met across the table.

I served the traditional turkey dinner with all the trimmings, and as usual, we all managed to over-indulge ourselves with too much good food, wine, and dessert. There was the typical camaraderie around the table and football games on television. The weather was pleasant, and my grandchildren were happily playing in the yard, enjoying the beautiful day. But even with all the usual sounds and activities going on around me, I still felt like something was missing.

Lately, I had noticed several new residents on Mom's wing. They were a whole new cast of characters, and things could get quite lively at times! There was one gentleman by the name of Larry, who tried to sell me his wheelchair each time I came to visit my mother. It was quite amusing when he continued to "hard sell" me on the standard features of the chair which included: great gas mileage, a comfortable seat, and guaranteed to fit in the trunk of any car. I tried to keep a straight face as I politely told him I would consider his offer and get back to him soon. With a triumphant expression, he quickly headed back to his room and promised to return with his business card. I could only imagine what he used to do for a living! As time went on, I got to know many of these residents and looked forward to seeing them. Many of them did not get visitors and seemed lonely. It really was heartbreaking.

With the approaching holidays, I was especially busy with Christmas activities, taking my dad to his numerous doctor visits, and learning more about all his growing health issues. I decided to take an active role in my father's health care by closely watching his diet and cooking healthy meals to improve his health. I have always felt strongly about proper nutrition and the amazing effects it has on our health and well-being.

My father's physician wholeheartedly agreed with me. After getting consistent reports of improved health after each doctor's visit, I couldn't deny the pride and sense of accomplishment I felt. I knew this was something I wanted to pursue, not just to help my father, but to share with others as well. Especially, my new community of friends!

Feeling encouraged, I made the decision to go back to school and learn more about nutrition and natural health care. I was never one to sit idle for too long, and I was starting to feel restless with the need to do more with my life. I knew it wouldn't be easy with everything else I was dealing with, but I believed in the long run, it would be well worth it. I had long considered changing careers but had never gotten serious about it. Since so much about my life had already changed, I figured this would be a perfect time to pursue a new career.

I began researching many different schools and opted for online education. After much consideration, I chose a program that was flexible and would work with my crazy schedule. It was finally official! At the start of the new year, I would begin studying for a whole new career. It felt so good to be taking control of my life again.

With December's arrival, the weather turned bitterly cold. There was a nasty virus going around, and many people at Elms Village became ill. When my mother started to develop a slight cough, I became worried and alerted staff. A few days later, she was running a low-grade fever, and her cough had become much worse. The doctor made his rounds and examined my mother. She had a slight rattle in her chest, but he didn't seem overly concerned.

Late the next evening, a nurse called to inform me that my mother was being taken to the hospital for a chest x-ray. When I told her that I would meet them at the hospital, she quickly explained that it would be a short visit unless they found something serious enough to keep her there. I then asked her to have someone call me as soon as they learned the results of her x-ray. I decided not to call my dad this late in the evening and needlessly worry him, especially when I didn't have much more information.

Early the next morning, I finally received a call from the doctor. He told me that my mother had a slight case of bacterial pneumonia, but that wasn't the only thing that was concerning him. The chest x-ray also revealed that she had an enlarged heart. He explained that he wanted to run more tests once my mother was feeling better, to determine the cause. In the meantime, they would treat my mother with antibiotics to help her with the viral symptoms.

I was rather shocked to hear this, but I agreed with him, and he said we would be in touch. After speaking with the doctor, I immediately called my dad to tell him what I had just learned. He was as surprised as I was, but we both knew that she was being well cared for. I went to visit my mother later that day, just as she was waking up from her afternoon nap. The nurse reported that she hadn't eaten much, but they were encouraging her to drink more fluids to stay hydrated. She still seemed a little groggy, but I grabbed her water glass and straw and decided to give it a try.

Once she was sitting up in her recliner chair, I put the straw to her lips. She just sat there, staring straight ahead and refused to drink any water. I coaxed her and even tried sweet-talking her, to no avail. Suddenly, I had an idea. I asked the nurse for some apple juice and a clear plastic glass. I remembered that my mother used to enjoy an occasional beer, and she and I would often split one.

When I asked my mother if she would like to split a beer with me, she eagerly nodded her head and said yes! I kept my fingers crossed and poured some apple juice into the glass. She took a sip through the straw and smiled and said that it was good beer! To everyone's surprise, she drank the whole can of juice. The nurses thought it was quite amusing, but we all agreed that we would continue to do whatever was necessary to keep her hydrated.

Several days later, the doctor announced that he felt my mother had recovered from her illness, and he was ready to order some tests on her heart. By the end of the week, we had the test results. Much to our dismay, my mother was diagnosed with congenital heart failure. It was yet another strike against us!

CHAPTER 15

For everything there is a season

As Christmas drew closer, everything seemed to take on a festive quality. There were holiday decorations, Christmas music, and decorated trees everywhere. One day I noticed that all the residents' doors had a Christmas decoration with their names on it. My mother happened to have an angel on her door, and for some reason, it held significant meaning for me. Lately, I had a strange fascination with angels, and it seemed like I noticed them everywhere!

For Christmas that year, I decided to give my mother a beautiful blue velvet pants outfit. I carefully put her name on the inside, even though it seemed that her roommate Ellen ended up sharing many of my mother's clothes. Honestly, I felt sorry for her since she didn't have any children of her own, and very few visitors. On occasion, I would sit and visit with Ellen while waiting for my mother to finish her shower or her physical therapy session. She was such a sweet lady!

On Christmas Eve day, my father, Randy and I decided to visit my mother. We were pleased to find that she was in a very receptive mood that day. She seemed to enjoy our company and was very excited to open her Christmas gifts. She loved everything we gave her and insisted on wearing her new blue velvet pants outfit right away!

The aide came in and helped my mother change into her new clothes. They fit perfectly, and she just sat there and smiled. I was admiring her new outfit when something shiny on the floor caught my eye. The silver cross pendant that I had given her for Mother's Day a few years ago had broken and fallen off. I picked it up and put it in my pocket before she noticed it was missing. I remembered how much the cross symbol meant to her and how she loved wearing it around her neck. I thought that I would just replace the broken chain and bring it back right after the holidays were over. Somehow, that never made it to the top of my to-do list!

When it was time for us to leave, she became distraught and begged us to stay with her. She grabbed my hand and pleaded with me not to go. I told her I would come back soon, and she started to cry. I sat with her for a few more moments and reminded her about the fancy meal the kitchen was preparing for her and all of her friends. That seemed to calm her down until we tried to leave again. We all gave her a big hug and told her how much we loved her. As we walked out the door, she looked mournful. By the time we got to the parking lot, I was overcome with emotion and tears filled my eyes. I couldn't help but think that this could very well be her last Christmas with us.

The old feelings of hurt and anger toward my mother had by this time softened significantly. Things were certainly different now, and I had a whole new perspective about my relationship with her. I no longer felt threatened, and she seemed so fragile and vulnerable that all I could think about was how to protect and care for her.

The next day was Christmas, and I tried not to let thoughts of my mother put a damper on the holiday. As usual, my house was filled with family, food, and presents. I kept imagining my mom sitting in the facility's dining room, missing her family. I decided to call the nurse's station and see if they could put my mother on the phone. The nurse on duty said she would check and see if she was available to speak and placed me on hold. She came back a few moments later and said my mother had just lain down for a nap. I thanked her for checking and hung up.

Once again, I felt like I was mourning the loss of my mother, even though she was just a short distance away. The holidays were bittersweet that year, and I was constantly reminded of how fleeting our time together was. I sadly remembered my youth and Christmases past, when the holiday would be ruined by my mother's bad behavior, and I had despised her for it. I felt cheated and couldn't wait for the day to end. Now, I felt a twinge of guilt as I pushed the memories from my mind.

The New Year arrived without much incident. I started my new classes and got right down to business. I soaked up everything like a sponge. Even though both of my parents were keeping me very busy, I still managed to fit in my class time and homework assignments. It was exciting to learn new things, and I had a particular interest in managing health issues with the foods we eat. I was even learning how to cook differently and make healthier changes to some of my favorite recipes.

Just a few days later, Randy called me on my cell phone just as I was leaving the nursing home. He sadly explained that his mother had taken a turn for the worse. She had been battling a terminal illness for the past several years and was not expected to survive much longer. Since my mother-in-law lived in Bismarck, that meant a trip to North Dakota we hadn't planned to take, especially during the cold, snowy month of January. To complicate matters, our second grandchild was due very soon, and it was important to Carisa that I be in the delivery room when she gave birth.

After checking in with my daughter, who luckily was not showing any signs of labor just yet, we packed a suitcase and headed to Bismarck. I also made sure the nursing home, as well as my father, knew how to reach me in case they needed to contact me for any reason.

We drove twelve straight hours before finally arriving at my brother-in-law's home, where we would be staying. Randy's two other siblings and their spouses were already at the hospital, and we immediately left to join them.

It was apparent that Randy's mother was fading fast, and we all said our tearful goodbyes. After nearly a week of taking turns holding a bedside vigil, she peacefully passed away. I couldn't help but admire the way Randy's family came together during times of crisis. It made me long for that kind of closeness within my own family. Over the years, we had slowly made amends with Randy's siblings, and eventually his parents.

Although the past was rarely talked about, we settled into what you would call a comfortable relationship. However, towards the end of my mother-in-law's life, I would like to think we became even closer as a family. Once we learned of my mother-in-law's illness, Randy and I both decided it was time to make peace with the past. Thankfully our relationship with my in-laws improved as my mother-in-law's illness progressed.

The funeral was going to be held early the following week, and I prayed that everything at home would wait until then. I continued to stay in touch daily with both my father and Carisa.

The weather was bitterly cold in Bismarck, which was typical for January. The day after the funeral, Randy and I, as well as his other two siblings, decided to head back home. Since we all lived in Colorado, we were going to caravan all the way back. Not long after we left, the roads started to ice over as the winds picked up and the temperatures dropped.

By the time we got to the South Dakota border, the visibility was near zero, and the main Interstate was closed due to poor travel conditions. Randy and I got to a nearby hotel first and managed to reserve two additional rooms for the others before they were all booked up by other stranded travelers.

As soon as we were settled, I quickly called home to let everyone know we would be delayed at least one more day due to the snowstorm. I was relieved to hear that there were still no incidents or changes, and everyone was doing well. By the next morning, the storm had passed, and the roads were cleared. It was slow going most of the way home until we got to Colorado, which was surprisingly untouched by snow.

One morning, not long after our trip, I woke up and felt miserable. With all the symptoms I was having, it was evident that I had a horrible case of the flu. As it so happened, I had a busy day, which included: finishing an essay for my class, taking Dad to the grocery store, picking up his medications, and his usual doctor's visit. I also had plans to visit my mother later that day. I knew it was a long shot, but I decided to call Shawn and see if he could help. He answered the phone almost immediately and seemed surprised to hear from me. I explained my predicament and asked if he could at least help with Dad.

He told me his schedule was full for the day, and when I asked if his wife could possibly help, his only excuse was that she had to pick up their daughter from school. I was getting more irritated by the minute as my stomach churned and my head pounded. I decided to reschedule my dad's doctor appointment and arranged for my son to take him grocery shopping and stop by the pharmacy that evening when he got home from work. I knew it was time to have that meeting with my brother that I had been putting off. So far, I had done everything to help care for our parents and gotten absolutely no support from him. Even though I had never known Shawn to be particularly generous when it came to offering assistance, I had hoped for a different response since it was our parents who needed help. With that, I rolled over and slept for the rest of the day.

After two days of moping around the house, I was finally starting to get my strength back. I took my dad to his rescheduled appointment, then to the grocery store. I filled his refrigerator with healthy meals that would keep him well fed for the rest of the week. After that, I went to Elms Village to talk with Nancy about my mother's progress. She reported that my mother had been sleeping a lot more lately, but with her condition, that was to be expected. After our meeting, I peeked my head inside my mother's doorway and saw that she was quietly sitting in her chair, just staring at the wall.

When I walked in, I greeted her with a big hug. As I stood back, I noticed that she seemed unaware of my presence, with no sign of emotion on her face. I sat with her for a few moments making small talk, but when she tried to respond, she struggled to get the words out. After several minutes, she just gave up in frustration. Everything she said sounded like gibberish. The aide finally came in and helped her to lie down for a nap. Feeling tired and emotionally drained, I decided to leave and call it a day.

That night, I was startled awake when my phone rang on the bedside table. I squinted at the clock, and it blared 2:05 a.m. When I picked up the phone, I heard Carisa's trembling voice telling me that she had gone into labor and would meet me at the hospital. I jumped into action and quickly got dressed. Barely awake, Randy mumbled, "Drive safely" as I gave him a quick kiss before heading out the door.

I got to the hospital in record time, several minutes before Carisa and her husband. My take-charge instincts kicked in, and I soon organized a small army of nurses and staff, who were waiting at the emergency room entrance with a wheelchair and paperwork in hand. A few moments later, my daughter arrived, and as soon as she was seated in the chair, she opened her mouth to say something and was suddenly overcome by a strong contraction. She was quickly wheeled up to labor and delivery, and less than two hours later, I was holding my precious grandson in my arms. It had been less than two weeks since my mother-in-law passed away, and as I gazed down into his tiny little face, I was reminded of how fragile life was.

I gave my daughter a warm hug and kissed my grandson goodbye before finally leaving the hospital. I felt such pride in being a grandmother, and I was immersed in warmth and tenderness as I drove home. I thought of my grandmother, and the joy and love she must have felt when her grandchildren were born. I suddenly realized the significance of the role I played and how it would affect generations to come.

Valentine's Day was coming up, and my dad, being the romantic guy that he was, wanted to do something special for my mother. I drove him to the store, and he decided to get a single red rose and a Valentine cookie that said, "I love you" on it. I got my usual vanilla coffee latte and planned to share it with my mother. We were heading down the hallway when we heard a loud commotion coming from her room. My mother was insisting that someone get her out of her chair because she thought she was late for an important appointment.

By the time we got to her room, she was pulling and tugging on the seat belt that was attached to her chair to prevent her from getting up on her own. She was a fall risk, and unfortunately, it was the only way to keep her safe. The nurse explained that she had been agitated all day and was getting angry with everyone. Dad tried to show her the rose and cookie that he had gotten for her, but she just ignored his efforts. She was obviously in a foul mood and didn't want anything to do with either one of us.

I located Nancy and suggested that maybe Mom had a urinary tract infection again. Every time she started acting like this, that usually seemed to be the culprit. Sure enough, the next day, I received a call explaining that my mother had indeed tested positive for another UTI. It was becoming more frequent with her, and the doctor thought that she was becoming immune to the antibiotics they were giving her to treat them. By the end of the week, the new antibiotics had finally taken effect, and she had calmed down considerably.

The following Saturday was my mother's birthday. It was hard to believe how much time had passed. As I reflected over the past year, the sorrow overwhelmed me. I remembered the woman she once was, a strong, vibrant—if scary—woman, the one I constantly measured myself by as a little girl. It was mortifying to see what she had been reduced to and since become. I could never have imagined how it would all turn out. My mother kept slipping further away from us. On some days, I felt as though she were already gone. I knew from past experience that if I let myself dwell on intense feelings for too long, they would eventually consume me. But instead of feeling depressed, I decided to pull myself together and celebrate another year of my mother's life surrounded by the people who loved her. I considered it another victory. It was time to plan a party!

CHAPTER 16

Diamonds are forever

I was thinking of my mother's birthday and wondering what to get her as a gift. I was doing some shopping on the Internet when I stumbled on a beautiful picture of an angel. I was so drawn to the image that I clicked on the website to find out more information about the artist. The picture I had been admiring was that of the Archangel Raphael, the angel of "healing." The description said that the artist behind this beautiful painting was blessed with a very special talent. She was able to create inspirational angel artwork that supports a calming, healing environment wherever it is placed. Each individual painting was blessed and was thought to inspire healing of the mind, body, and spirit.

I was so fascinated by this beautiful piece of artwork that I knew in an instant; it was the perfect gift for my mother. I imagined just the right spot on the wall to hang the picture, right beside her bed. It would be the first thing she saw when she woke up, and I hoped it would bring her comfort and peace. I also purchased a beautiful white and gold frame that would set off the vibrant colors in the painting.

Just as I did the year before on her birthday, I reserved the special occasion room for my mother's party. I baked her favorite cake, and the facility kitchen supplied the coffee and soft drinks. After everyone sang happy birthday, I offered my mother a piece of cake. I suddenly noticed how tired and frail she looked. She barely touched her cake. As I observed her aging features, it was evident that life had taken its toll. Her once-pretty face had lost its luster; her smooth porcelain skin was now etched with lines. The striking blue eyes, one of her best features, looked empty and faded now. Her chestnut hair had turned completely white. Looking at earlier photos, it was hard to imagine that this was the same person.

Shortly after opening her last present, she fell asleep in her chair. I took her back to her room, and the aide helped her lie down for a nap. I stood back and admired the beautiful angel painting on the wall beside her bed. It was truly mesmerizing! I only hoped it would have the same effect on my mother as it did on me.

After checking on my mother one last time, I went back to the party room to help clean up. Shawn was still sitting at the table, drinking a cup of coffee. It was time to schedule our meeting. It was now or never. I casually grabbed a cup of coffee and pulled up a chair across from him. I put on my best sister smile and gently asked if we could get together sometime soon, just the two of us. He looked at me suspiciously and asked what I wanted to talk about. I didn't want to get into the subject with him at that moment, so I just invited him to come over and discuss some things that had been on my mind lately. He seemed reluctant but agreed to call me later that week.

By the end of the week, there was still no word from my brother. I knew this was not going to be an easy task, but I was determined to have that talk with him if it was the last thing I did! I picked up the phone and dialed his number. He answered just before it went into voice mail. I politely reminded him of my invitation, and he finally agreed to come to my house that evening.

I really wanted our meeting to go well, so I bought some wine and his favorite beer. When Shawn arrived, he had a sour look on his face, and I tried not to let it discourage me. I poured us both a drink, and we made small talk before getting to the main topic. As soon as I brought up the subject of caring for our parents, he immediately became angry and defensive. I tried my best to stay calm and explained that I would appreciate his help and support in the matter. With that, he set down his glass and headed for the door. When I asked him why he was acting this way, he angrily replied, "You signed up for this, I didn't!"

After he slammed the door, I just stood there in shock and disbelief. I was absolutely flabbergasted! How could Shawn be so cold? Never in my wildest dreams would I have imagined that my own brother could do this to his family. I discussed it with Randy later that day as I tried to wrap my head around the whole concept. Although I was extremely grateful for my own family's love and support, nothing could take the place of a sibling to share the ups and downs of caring for your parents. I was left to face the fact that my only sibling had abandoned me. I had considered that Shawn was in the midst of his career and had recently started a family, but the facts of the matter remained. They were his parents too.

Because I was the eldest child and also female, I believe it was assumed that caring for our aging parents would fall to me. I often wondered what would have happened if I had refused to take on the responsibility to care for them. Many times, I asked myself the undeniable question: "Why had I chosen to do this?" Did it come from a sense of duty, or perhaps something much deeper? I had given up so much already. Not only did I miss out on having a normal childhood, but now my adulthood was compromised as well. Not to mention my fears about the future, my finances, and the new career I hoped to one day have.

As much as I tried to stay optimistic, there were days I struggled with these thoughts, especially during times of isolation, loneliness, and even self-pity. Although Randy was usually a good sport about all the unexpected situations that arose, which usually led to missed vacations and last-minute cancelations, it put a strain on our marriage and added stress to our daily lives.

At the end of the day, however, it was my unshakeable faith in God and the support and friendship of other struggling caregivers that helped me persevere and prevented me from sinking further into the darkness.

Several months went by without one word from my brother. I guess I still secretly hoped that he would come to his senses and realize how badly we needed him. My parents' fiftieth wedding anniversary was just a month away. Under normal circumstances, we would have had a big celebration for my parents. But life was anything but normal these days! I talked with my father about it, and we both agreed that keeping things simple would be the best way to celebrate.

As my parents' anniversary drew near, my dad announced that he had an idea. He said that he had always wanted to get my mother a larger diamond for her wedding ring, but somehow never got around to it. He thought this would be the perfect opportunity. We kept my mother's original wedding ring at my father's apartment for safekeeping. The nursing home had warned us that they could not be held responsible for anything valuable if it was lost or stolen. With that in mind, dad decided to buy her a beautiful cubic zirconium ring.

One day after my father's doctor appointment, we went to the jewelry store to look at rings. After looking at several styles, he ended up picking out a beautiful three-stone ring with lots of sparkle! It was a gorgeous ring, even if the diamonds weren't real. They sized it according to her original wedding ring and placed it in a blue velvet box. Dad just beamed and looked like a young man who was ready to propose!

Even though I knew it would be tense, I thought Shawn should at least be included in our small celebration for our parents. I decided to send him an email and invite him and his wife. I wasn't surprised when a week later, there was still no response from him. I mentioned it to my dad, and he said he would call Shawn himself and ask him to come.

That weekend, we planned to celebrate my parents' golden anniversary. Since they typically preferred a quiet evening at their favorite restaurant, a small gathering seemed fitting. When I asked my father if Shawn and his wife planned to attend, he said he wasn't sure and that Shawn told him he would think about it. I ordered a small cake for the special day and dug out my parents' wedding album and some old family photos. Elms Village let us use a small room for the occasion, and we decorated with a few streamers, balloons and flowers.

When we got to my mother's room, she was sitting in her chair wearing a big smile. I was surprised to see that moment of recognition on her face as I bent down to hug her. I asked her if she knew what day it was, and when I told her the month and date, she actually remembered that it was her wedding anniversary. We all just looked at each other in total disbelief!

We went to the designated room that the facility had reserved for us, and I set out the family photos. After waiting a reasonable amount of time, it was clear that Shawn had decided not to come. We went ahead with our plans, and Dad didn't waste any time. He took out the blue velvet box that contained my mother's ring. When he opened the lid, she just stared at it with wide eyes. He placed it on her finger, and it fit perfectly. She was so surprised that she was speechless for several moments. When she could finally speak, she announced that it was the most beautiful ring she had ever seen. My dad was pleased as punch!

After we had some cake, my mother was paging through the wedding album and smiling. She remembered every single person in the pictures and reminisced about funny things that happened on their wedding day. I learned a lot that afternoon as I listened to stories that I had never even heard before. I laughed at the thought of their friends short- sheeting the bed on their wedding night, and my dad pushing my mom around in a wheelbarrow on their honeymoon. Once again, we were blessed with a miracle that no one could explain. She had come back to share this very special day with us!

When the party was over, we walked my mother down the hallway back to her room. Along the way, she insisted on stopping several times so that she could show everyone her new ring. She was so proud of how "dazzling" it was, and Dad couldn't have been more pleased. It turned out to be a perfect day for both of my parents. The only thing that was missing, of course, was Shawn.

Over the next several days, my mother was blessed with clarity once more. Just like before, it was as if the dementia had literally disappeared! She couldn't stop admiring her new ring and said she felt like a queen. Every time my dad came to visit, they looked like newlyweds. Everyone enjoyed watching them together and mentioned how sweet it was.

Unfortunately, it was not meant to last. By the end of the week, Mom had no recollection at all and seemed more withdrawn than ever. It was the very last time my mother would ever experience the gift of clarity.

CHAPTER 17

Full circle

Over the next few weeks, Nancy reported that my mother was losing weight. Her appetite was decreasing, and she didn't seem to have much interest in food. She did, however, still request her favorite ice cream, rainbow sherbet! As long as she was getting some kind of nourishment, no one argued with her, and she could have as much as she wanted.

Between my father and me, one of us would try to visit at lunchtime to see if we could coax her into eating more of her meal. She would usually end up just staring at her plate or falling asleep. Since nothing seemed to work, we decided to give her supplemental nutrition drinks twice a day to keep her from completely withering away.

Summer was coming to an end, and the weather was turning colder. My mother was spending more time sleeping in her chair, so my father brought in one of her favorite throw blankets from his apartment to cover her and help keep her warm. On some days, we would both sit there with her, not saying a word, and just watch her sleep. Sometimes she would suddenly wake up with a surprised look on her face, as though something had startled her. Then she would peacefully nod off again. It was hard to say if she was dreaming or just distracted by something.

It was becoming a new pattern for her, and it was evident that she was entering the next stage of her illness. It was hard to determine when to come for a visit because you could never predict when she would be awake. One day I brought some old family pictures and a tape recorder with some of her favorite songs. When she heard the music playing, she opened her eyes and lifted her head. I looked at her and smiled, not knowing what to expect. I could tell by her eyes that she did not recognize me, but at least I was able to get a response from her. I showed her the family pictures and talked about the events and the people in them. She just smiled and nodded her head. If this was all I could do to connect with my mother now, I considered it to be quite an accomplishment. Instinctively I knew that things were rapidly changing, and I would have to find new ways to communicate with her. I wasn't ready to give up the battle just yet!

I noticed my mother was growing tired again, and I decided to pack it up and call it a day. As I was putting the old photos back in the box, one of them caught my eye. It was a picture of my mother holding me on her lap. She had her arms wrapped tightly around me. We were smiling broadly, and we both looked relaxed and happy. I was about three years old, and I recognized the Bear Tooth Pass behind us in the photo that was taken on a trip my parents had taken to the Yellowstone National Park.

As I looked more closely at the photograph, I realized that there weren't very many pictures of my mother and me together, even when I was young. It made me wonder—at what point did our lives take such a drastic turn? I realized that she must have tried her best to love me and be a good mother before she ultimately gave up on life. It was a sobering thought, and I couldn't imagine feeling that hopeless. I considered the close bond I felt with my children, and I suddenly had chills. It was disturbing to think of what could possibly cause a mother to reject her own child.

One afternoon, I came in for a visit, and Nancy stopped me in the hallway. She said my mother was refusing to take her medication, and some changes would have to be made. As I suspected, my mother's condition had significantly progressed. The medication she took to slow down her dementia and manage her Parkinson's disease was no longer effective. In fact, most of the pills she took were no longer managing her symptoms. We both agreed that it was best to stop giving her the medication. The only time she would receive any kind of medicine was to keep her comfortable.

Early on, both my parents signed a living will that specifically stated that certain kinds of medical treatment would not be given to prolong their natural lives. This fell into that category, and all I could do was respect those wishes.

I knew our time together was dwindling, and I was reminded of it each time I came to visit. On those rare occasions when my mother was fully coherent, I realized that she was now able to live in the present moment, something she was never able to do before her illness. As I sat there with her, holding her hand, I realized how much she had taught me throughout our lives. I thought about growing up without a mother's unconditional love and how I learned to love myself in spite of it. I had come to learn the value of family and people you hold closest to your heart. I also learned to be strong in the face of fear. But perhaps the toughest lesson of all was learning about forgiveness.

We had once been a family divided by heartbreak. And now, we were reunited by love and unforeseen circumstances. I was beginning to understand that there is a reason for everything that happens to us and was reminded again that God works in mysterious ways!

Even though we had a troubled and turbulent past, our time together now had so much more meaning. Every moment was infinitely more precious. I thought back to a time not so long ago when I didn't want to speak with my mother, or even be in the same room. I remembered when I refused to accept her apologies, and especially the times I told her I hated her. I cringed as I pushed away those awful memories. Living in the moment was what was important now, for both of us.

Our mother-daughter relationship was what brought us here together in the first place. It was proof that love can survive and withstand anything if you are willing. From the very beginning, she was a powerful influence in my life. I could feel the time slipping by, stealing my mother away from me. I had spent so many nights wondering what my life would be like after she was gone. Somehow, I convinced myself that knowing about the impending future would help prepare me for the end. Now that the end was getting closer, I wondered if I was prepared after all. Is there really such a thing as being prepared when someone you love dies? I couldn't seem to imagine how different the world would be without the one who gave me the gift of life itself.

I glanced over at my mother, who had fallen asleep as I was getting lost in my thoughts. I gazed at the angel artwork above my mother's bed and said a silent prayer, hoping it would bring peace and comfort. I thought about how unpredictable life could be. My mother and I had spent so many years in a dysfunctional relationship, and the very thing that would inevitably take her away from us was what brought us together again. I felt like I was already grieving for her on a daily basis. The only thing that made any sense to me was my firm belief that this was God's divine plan for us both.

I wondered about my brother Shawn, and how he was handling all of this. Was he feeling the same emotions that I was? Were we really so different from each other in how we dealt with these difficult situations? I wanted to reach out to him, but I just didn't have the strength anymore. Even my father seemed somewhat distant, although I knew that he cared deeply for his family. We were all coping in our own way and doing the best we could.

It finally occurred to me that my mother was the only one who was blissfully unaware of this whole situation. Or was she? Even though she seemed completely oblivious to it all, she was content in her own peaceful little world. It was almost as if she had accepted her fate. Maybe this was God's way of sustaining us until the very end, so we didn't have to suffer from all that inner turmoil. Suddenly I had hope!

When I stood up to leave, I kissed my mother goodbye and told her how much I loved her. As I drove home, I was still deep in thought, and I felt a weight being lifted off my shoulders. If she could accept this, I could too. We were going to get through this together. I was starting to believe this was God's ultimate plan. We were blessed with so much love; how could I be anything but accepting?

There are no guarantees in life, no matter how much control we think we have. I believe that we are given a choice of how we react to life's circumstances, and we must live with those choices, wherever they may lead. By accepting the inevitable, we put ourselves in God's hands, which brings us closer to our life's purpose. With this, we are rewarded with peace and comfort.

I felt I had found the answers that I needed to get through this ordeal. Maybe there really was healing inspiration in that angel artwork on my mother's wall! I was learning to trust and have faith in my life as never before. I got the feeling that we had closed a significant gap in our lives, and we were finally able to come full circle.

CHAPTER 18

Swept away

Fall was in the air, and I was busy with my classes and spending as much quality time as I could with my grandchildren. Life seemed to have taken on a whole new meaning. It had a profound effect on me as I observed it through new eyes. I thought more about my own mortality these days, and the direction my life had taken. Life's events certainly have a way of changing us and can even include a few opportunities if we choose to perceive them as such.

The holidays would be here again soon, and I realized how different they would be this year. I was almost certain this would be my mother's last year with us. And not only that, Shawn and I were no longer on speaking terms. I told myself that maybe it was better this way, but it still dampened my spirits.

It was an unusually warm day, and Indian summer was hanging on well into November. I loved this time of year; it always made me feel happy and a little nostalgic. I decided to put my homework aside and pay my mother a visit at Elms Village. When I got to her room, she was fast asleep in her bed. It was already late morning, and she was still in her nightgown. When I tried to wake her, she didn't stir. I spoke louder, but she still refused to wake up. I realized she was in a very deep slumber. I stood there watching her chest gently move up and down with each breath.

I looked for the nurse to find out what was going on with my mother. When I finally got a chance to speak with her, she told me that my mother had been like this all day, so they had decided to let her sleep. They were, however, planning to get her dressed shortly and take her to the dining room for lunch. I decided to stay and see if I could get her to wake up long enough to eat something.

When we got to the dining room, she was still barely awake. I tried to get her to eat her lunch, but she wouldn't open her mouth. I encouraged her to drink some juice through a straw, but she only took a few sips. After an hour, it was apparent I was not going to get her to eat anything. I took her back to her room. All she wanted to do was sleep.

I brushed her hair and spoke softly to her as she quietly dozed in her chair. I decided to sit there with her a while longer and see if she would eventually wake up. I looked out the window and watched children playing on the playground at the school across the street. It seemed almost contradictory watching life go by from the stark contrast of my mother's quiet room.

I waited a while longer, but she still wouldn't wake up. The aide put her back into bed to finish her nap. As I drove home, I rolled down the window to let in the warm breeze. I enjoyed the earthy scent of fall in the air and noticed the beautiful colored leaves as I drove along the now-familiar street. I thought back to the years before when I would look forward to this time of year. Now, I almost dreaded the changing seasons. It meant that I would be forced to keep moving forward and be swept away by the current that eventually brings us all to our inevitable end.

When I got home, I thought about working on my class assignments to take my mind off things. I had just gotten my books out when the phone rang. The caller ID said Elms Village was calling. I thought it was odd since I had just left there and felt a bit anxious when I answered the phone. My mother's doctor asked if I had some time to speak with her. I immediately agreed, and I couldn't help but notice the seriousness of her tone. A chill ran down my spine as I braced myself for bad news.

We discussed my mother's recent progression with Parkinson's disease and dementia. She also explained that it was very normal for my mother to lose her interest in food and spend more time sleeping. Even though I knew all these things were true, I was not prepared for what came next.

The doctor gently told me that it was time to consider hospice care. My mother could still stay at Elms Village, but a hospice team would take over her primary care. Then she carefully explained that hospice care only became necessary when it was believed that the patient had only six months or less to live. I could barely breathe. I had already read all the pamphlets and educated myself about the details of hospice care. But those two words, *hospice care*, made it all seem too real. Before hanging up, I managed to set up a meeting with the new hospice team for the following day.

After those words sunk in, I realized I would have to pull myself together before calling my father with this latest news. I wasn't sure how I would get the words out without completely falling apart. I decided to take my dogs for a short walk, hoping to clear my head and burn off some of the intensity. I walked around my neighborhood for about an hour, keeping a swift pace and focusing on the crunching of the leaves and my dogs' enthusiasm. Eventually, I started to calm down. By the time I got home, I was feeling much better. The fresh air and exercise had done me a world of good.

I poured myself a tall glass of iced tea as I dialed my father's phone number. We chatted for a bit and commented on the warm weather we were having. Then I slowly told him about the day's events at the nursing home and the phone conversation I had earlier with the doctor. He was as shocked as I was, but not entirely surprised by the news. When I mentioned the appointment with hospice the next day, he agreed to come.

The appointment was scheduled for ten o'clock that morning. The weather had turned colder, and the sky looked gloomy and gray. It certainly reflected my mood as I drove to Dad's apartment to pick him up before the meeting. When we got to Elms Village, we were told by the receptionist to meet the hospice worker in the small meeting room in the back of the front lobby. As we sat there waiting, Dad and I made small talk, carefully avoiding the subject of why we were there.

A few moments later, a pleasant young man came in and introduced himself as Adam. He handed out folders that contained information about hospice care and went over the entire process with us. By the time we finished, I felt completely overwhelmed. He said he wanted to make some changes by first replacing my mother's geriatric chair. Then he would go through the list of medications that she was still taking, although by this time there weren't many.

After the meeting, we headed down the hallway to my mother's room. When we walked in, I was glad to see that my mother was awake and seemed alert. He politely introduced himself to her and explained that he would be taking very good care of her from now on. She just smiled and nodded her head in agreement. Then he said that he would be right back. A few minutes later, he returned with a new chair. As I observed it closely, I agreed that it looked like a suitable chair for my mother now that she slept more during the day. It reclined and allowed her to relax or doze more comfortably and would prevent her from staying in bed all day. We discussed a few more details, and by the time we left, I had to admit, I was feeling a little better about the idea of hospice care.

On the way back to Dad's apartment, we discussed telling the rest of the family about my mother's new situation. I agreed to tell my children as well as other close family members, and my father said he would break the news to Shawn.

Two days later, I received a phone call from Adam, my mother's new hospice nurse. He explained that she was continuing to lose weight and suspected that she had another urinary tract infection. I was surprised at this last bit of information because she usually became very feisty at the onset of a UTI. We again discussed my mother's living will, and her wishes about receiving medical treatment. We both agreed that she would only be given whatever was necessary to keep her comfortable.

After we hung up, I started to wonder how much time my mother had left. Then I began to worry about her final days and wanted to make sure that she wouldn't be alone when she passed. There was so much to think about, and I tried to keep things in perspective. I really wished I could talk to Shawn about these things. I felt that it was important for my mother to have her family intact before she left this world.

CHAPTER 19
All things are possible

The Christmas season was upon us once again, but my heart wasn't in it. I was finding it hard, if not impossible, to concentrate on my schoolwork, and had absolutely no desire to get involved with any holiday festivities this year. I realized my emotions were getting the best of me, so I decided to start keeping a journal. There is just something so therapeutic about putting pen to paper and writing down all your deepest thoughts and darkest fears. It provides a safe place to "put" them, rather than keeping them trapped and tumbling around in your head. I remembered hearing somewhere that writing in a journal is equivalent to having a session with a good therapist. In my case, this proved to be true.

For the sake of my family and because it was Christmas, I tried to keep everything as normal as possible. I went through the motions of decorating the tree, wrapping presents, and baking cookies. I decided against sending out my usual holiday letter because I just couldn't seem to come up with any happy news to write about. Everything seemed to revolve around my mother these days.

One afternoon I got in the car and drove to Elms Village. I couldn't help but notice the beautiful decorations, twinkling lights, and large Christmas tree in the front lobby. As I opened the door to my mother's room, I recognized the same angel that had been there the previous year, only this time it was taped to the closet door that faced her bed. She was sitting in her chair and seemed to be staring intently at the angel. When I mentioned it, she pointed at it and smiled. I told her it must be her guardian angel that was watching over her. She just nodded her head and continued to gaze at the angel as though completely amazed by its presence. I must admit that watching her do this gave me goosebumps!

Just then, the nurse came in and reported that my mother was still eating very little at mealtime. Since she rarely refused a bowl of her favorite ice cream, we both agreed that it was more important to get some nourishment in her, even if it meant letting her eat all the rainbow sherbet she wanted. The nurse came back a few moments later with a bowl of ice cream, and sure enough, my mother finished every last bite! Feeling satisfied that my mother was not going to go hungry that day, I decided to head home.

I had only been home for five minutes when the phone rang. I recognized Cory's phone number on the caller ID and picked up immediately, always happy to talk with him. He had gotten home early from work that day and obviously had something on his mind that he wanted to discuss with me. I was surprised and somewhat taken aback when he asked me if I had made amends with my brother. My son had always been fond of his uncle Shawn, and I knew he was concerned about our current situation with my mother, just as we all were.

I admitted that I had not spoken with Shawn in several months, nor did I have any plans to do so. Cory had always seemed older than his years and genuinely wanted to help in any way he could. It didn't come as much of a surprise when he said that he was going to talk to his uncle Shawn and try to get him to make peace with the family. "After all," he said, "it is Christmas!" I certainly couldn't argue with him there.

Cory was on a mission, and I knew there was no talking him out of it. I wished him luck but told him not to get his hopes up. After we hung up, I couldn't help but feel a sense of pride that my son was willing to take matters into his own hands. I just hoped it wouldn't make things worse than they already were. I wasn't sure what would happen, but I prayed that maybe, just maybe, we could all be a family in time for Christmas.

That evening, Cory called to tell me that he had indeed spoken with Shawn and his wife, and it went surprisingly well. He said that my brother was willing to talk to me, but only if I called him. I said I would have to think about it and told Cory how proud of him I was. I knew it meant a lot to him to have the whole family together, not just for Christmas but also in a larger sense.

When we hung up, I talked to Randy about the situation, and we both agreed on how important it was to be a family during this time. I went upstairs and dialed Shawn's number, not quite knowing what to say. When he answered the phone, I got the feeling that he was expecting my call. Feeling encouraged, I started to tell him how glad I was that we could finally talk and get everything straightened out. He didn't answer right away and finally said, "I really think we should just hit the reset button and move on."

Feeling more than a little disappointed, I reluctantly agreed. It wasn't quite what I had in mind, but considering our current situation, it was better than not speaking at all. Ever since my parents moved to Colorado, our relationship had slowly become more distant, almost to the point of being non-existent. No matter how many times I brought up the subject with my brother, it always fell on deaf ears. I eventually gave up and learned to accept it.

After discussing my mother's condition and contemplating what would come next, I decided to invite him, his wife, and three-year-old daughter over for Christmas dinner. He agreed to come, and after we hung up, I felt an odd combination of relief and frustration. I was relieved that we were speaking again, but frustrated that nothing had been resolved. I decided to look on the bright side and consider it a small victory in the big scheme of things.

After turning on the holiday music and Christmas lights, I suddenly felt lighter. I realized we were far from perfect, but as long as we were a family, there was hope, and we would face the future together.

With only one week left to go, I figured it was time to start planning Christmas dinner. I poured myself a glass of wine and got out my favorite holiday recipes. I dug out one of my mother's old cookbooks and decided to look for some old family favorites. As I was paging through the book,

I recognized my mother's neat cursive handwriting beside some of the recipes, and it brought tears to my eyes. She had obviously made her own notes to reflect the alterations she made. I thought of all the times she tried so hard to cook a good meal or try a new recipe. Although my mother wasn't what you would call a great cook, I believe she always tried her best to make something special.

The next morning, I told my father what had happened between Shawn and me the night before. He was deeply touched and admitted how much it meant to him that we would be spending Christmas together as a family. As the holiday drew closer, I realized that I had been secretly dreading it this year. Deep down, I knew this would be my mother's last Christmas with us, and I couldn't help but think about all the time we wasted being angry at each other over the years. Time was so precious now, and I just wanted it to last forever!

Early on Christmas Eve, my father and I went to visit my mother and bring her our Christmas gifts. When we rounded the corner of the hallway, I immediately caught a glimpse of her in the dining room where there was a choir singing Christmas carols. As we got closer, I could see the look of emotion on her face as she took in the familiar words to "O Holy Night." As I sat down next to her, she was utterly absorbed in the music and didn't seem to notice that Dad and I had arrived.

As we listened together, I, too, got caught up in the moment and was completely immersed in the meaning of that beautiful song. When I heard the words from the third verse: *"Truly he taught us to love one another; His law is Love, and His gospel is Peace,"* I felt as though those simple words were being spoken directly to me. This journey with my family had taught me more about unconditional love than anything in this world ever could have. I finally understood that this was a *divine* experience if I chose to embrace it. Even though this was my mother's very last Christmas, we had been given the biggest gift of all. Love! Pure unconditional love! It was time to make peace with the past and be grateful for the opportunity before us. Some people never get that chance, and I realized just how blessed we were at this very moment!

By the time the song ended, I had tears in my eyes. When I turned to look at my mother, I was surprised to see that she did too. I knew she was still very much with us, and I could only imagine what was going on in her mind at that moment. Dad and I took her back to her room and helped her open her gifts. I got her some warm slippers and dad got her a beautiful angel plaque with one of her favorite bible verses engraved on it. She seemed tired out after all the afternoon activities, and it was almost dinnertime by then.

That night as we celebrated Christmas, I was overcome with a feeling of an almost otherworldly intervention that made all things possible. Instead of dreading the holiday, I decided to celebrate the miracle that happened on this night so long ago and reminded myself again that we are all brought together for *His* purpose.

CHAPTER 20

Between worlds

It was a bitterly cold January morning. The holidays were over, and a new year had begun. I decided to buckle down and try to concentrate on my classes. I had been putting things off lately, and now I had to make up for it. The light snow outside gave me a cozy feeling, and I was thankful to be home on a day like this. I had just gotten my second cup of coffee and was headed upstairs to my home office to get some work done when the phone rang.

I recognized the phone number and immediately answered it. The hospice nurse was calling to let me know that my mother had developed a cough that was somewhat concerning. He also added that she had a slight temperature and asked for my permission to do a chest x-ray. After asking a few more questions, I readily agreed to the x-ray as well as some aspirin. He promised to call with the results as soon as they were back.

As I hung up the phone, I tried not to worry. The peaceful, cozy feeling I had earlier had all but disappeared. I got out my books and began typing up a long-overdue essay for one of my classes. I tried to concentrate, but thoughts of my mother kept running through my mind. What if this was serious? What if she didn't recover from this? I couldn't seem to stop the constant chatter in my head.

Somehow, I managed to finish the essay just as Adam called back with the results. He told me she had fluid on her left lung, and her respiratory signs were more than a little concerning, especially since she had congestive heart failure. He felt it was necessary to consult with the doctor and said again that he would be in touch. As soon as we hung up, I called my father. After discussing it, we decided to go and visit my mother together.

When we got there, she was in her bed, resting comfortably. The nurse had just taken her vital signs, and her temperature was normal again. After she left, Dad and I each pulled up a chair and sat next to her bed. She appeared to be in a deep sleep, and all we could do was be there with her. I reached for her hand, and it felt so small and frail. As I gazed at my mother while she slept, I was acutely aware of how much she seemed to have shrunk. The twin-sized bed almost seemed too large for her small, thin body. Her disease had completely taken over and ravaged what was left of her.

We were just about to leave when Adam and the doctor came into the room. We waited patiently while the doctor examined my mother. When he finished, he had a vague expression on his face. He told us that she had entered end-stage heart failure, and her symptoms would only continue to progress. He further explained that this most likely accounted for her lack of appetite, excessive sleeping, and persistent cough.

After he left the room, Dad and I sat back down next to my mother's bed, both of us feeling the weight of the doctor's words. There wasn't much left to say, but it was oddly comforting to just sit there in stony silence, lost in our own thoughts.

That evening I called Shawn to tell him of the day's events. He was concerned as the rest of us were, and yet the news wasn't quite so surprising. After all, we knew this was coming. After I hung up the phone, I realized how much I had missed talking with my brother. I was grateful to be sharing this emotional experience with my only sibling, especially now. Things were only going to get worse from here!

My mother seemed to wither away a little more each day. On one particular visit, however, I was surprised to find her in a very feisty mood. The nurse was trying her best to get her to drink some fluids, but she was having none of it. I offered to give it a try, but as soon as I put the straw to her mouth, she immediately slapped it out of my hand. The cup flew across the room, making a huge mess all over the floor. A staff member quickly came in with a mop to clean it up. As soon as I tried to move my mother's wheelchair out of the way, she started cursing and swearing at me as if she didn't know me.

I tried to calm her down, but she just looked me right in the eye and said, "Your hair is such a mess, and I'm sure people must tease you!" Her comment was so absurd, and I was so surprised that I burst out laughing and suddenly, she was laughing too. I wasn't quite sure if she was laughing with me or at me, but either way, it was good to hear her laugh again even if it was at my expense!

The days that followed varied from one extreme to the other. On certain days Mom was sleepy and barely coherent, and on other days she was full of surprises. I was genuinely amazed by the constant change in her character. In fact, she almost seemed to be enjoying herself. At times she would suddenly begin laughing at something, or possibly someone, that only she could see. Sometimes she looked as though she were interacting with another person, even though she was alone in the room.

One day I walked into her room, and she asked me if I would bring the ball back so she could finish playing her game with the little boy. When I asked her who the little boy was, she said it was Jason. I felt a chill run down my spine at the mention of my late brother's name. I suddenly remembered hearing stories about people close to death, who communicated with their deceased loved ones.

I gave myself a mental shake and reasoned that confusion, disorientation, and hallucinations were all common symptoms of her disease. But even as I told myself this, I wasn't totally convinced. When these episodes became more frequent and started to include others, such as her late mother and father, it certainly left me wondering!

At other times she seemed very serene, gazing off into the distance to a place only she could see. Sometimes a faint smile would cross her lips, almost as though she were anticipating something pleasant in her mind's eye. One day she looked at my father very intently and said, "Do you know how handsome I always thought you were?" Before my father could even respond, she just turned her head and closed her eyes. She was completely unaware of the impact she had just made. My father suddenly stood up with tears in his eyes and quickly walked away to compose himself.

It was beginning to be quite obvious that some new changes were taking place, although I couldn't exactly explain what they were. When I mentioned all of this to Adam, he suggested bringing in a chaplain from the hospice team. I readily agreed and thought it was a good idea.

As it turned out, Eric, the hospice chaplain, was exactly what we needed. He was like a breath of fresh air! I immediately liked him, and I think my mother did too. He seemed to bring out the best in everyone. When I told him about these latest concerns, he didn't laugh or tell me that these things weren't really happening. In fact, he said it happened all the time!

After explaining this strange phenomenon, he assured me that this was a common occurrence. When the end of life draws closer, we are literally between worlds, and it can be extremely comforting to see our loved ones. He said the best thing to do is accept it and never try to dismiss or minimize the experience. He then added that trying to "correct" my mother could actually have a traumatizing effect on her.

By the time we were finished talking, I was feeling comforted by the idea that there were possibly loved ones standing by to help my mother make the transition from this world to the next. The only thing that left me with a sinking feeling was the fact that my mother was preparing to leave this world and her family. Of this, I was sure.

CHAPTER 21

Going home

I began thinking about my mother's birthday, which was coming up in March, just a few weeks away. I wanted to plan a special day for her, but something in the back of my mind prevented me from doing so. Lately, I had a strange feeling that I couldn't seem to shake. I decided to talk to Adam and ask him what his thoughts were on my mother's prognosis. He was somewhat optimistic and didn't appear to be too concerned about anything happening just yet. Even though I considered his words, and my mother didn't appear to be visibly dying at the moment, something just didn't feel quite right. Each time I thought about her birthday, my mind drew a complete blank. So instead, I decided to concentrate on my grandson's first birthday, which was coming up the following week.

There was a horrible case of the flu going around, and my father suddenly fell ill. He developed a deep cough, and I immediately took him to the clinic. The doctor sent us home with antibiotics, cough medicine, and orders to get plenty of rest. I again had to postpone my own personal agenda so I could care for my father and deal with my mother's issues as well. Going back and forth between both of my parents made for long days and left me completely worn out. By the next week, my father started to show signs of improvement, but the annoying cough hung on. We thought it was best for him to stay away from my mother, in case he was still contagious.

The strange feeling I had earlier that month was becoming more persistent, and I began to feel anxious. I visited my mother almost every day now, and I could sense an almost otherworldly aura around her. Something felt different, but I couldn't put my finger on it. One afternoon I was sitting with her when suddenly, her eyes lit up! It was almost as if someone familiar had just entered the room. I decided to throw caution to the wind and asked my mother who was in the room with us.

She slowly smiled and had such a look of tenderness on her face that it wasn't hard to guess who it was. The child she had never stopped longing for was here now, to help her find her way home. I suddenly realized that part of my anxiety stemmed from the great unknown. My mother's earthly capabilities were so limited that I worried what would become of her once she left this world. I had always believed in God and His kingdom, but now I felt as though my whole belief system was being tested.

Several days later, my mother's cough worsened, and I worried that she had gotten the flu that was going around. Adam ordered another chest x-ray and said that her lungs seemed clear and wasn't overly concerned at this point. When I came to visit my mother that morning, she was angry and obviously in a bad mood. She refused to eat and wouldn't let anyone touch her. In fact, I had set up an appointment for her that morning to get a haircut, and the poor beautician had all she could handle just trimming her bangs!

It was the end of the week, and I had a long list of things to do over the weekend. Early Saturday morning, Randy announced that he was going into the office to get some work done, and I was glad to have the house to myself. After he left, the house seemed eerily quiet. As I busied myself in the kitchen, I could hear the birds singing outside my window. I stopped what I was doing and gazed outside as fresh tears rolled down my cheeks. Suddenly I was overcome with a sense of urgency that was so intense I could barely breathe. I knew that I had to get to my mother! I got dressed, hopped in the car, and drove over to my father's apartment. I explained that I needed him to come with me, and he quickly agreed. By the time we got to my mother's wing, my heart was pounding so hard I felt dizzy.

Just then, I spotted her in the corner of the dining room. She was sitting in her wheelchair, completely slumped over. Her eyes were closed, and she appeared to be sleeping. When I tried to wake her, she didn't stir. As I touched her forehead, she felt warm and feverish. I called for the nurse, and she quickly took her vital signs. By the look on her face, I knew something was wrong. She told us that my mother had a high fever, and her blood pressure didn't look good.

With the help of an assistant, we got my mother back into her bed. The hospice nurse who was on call for the weekend was summoned, and he arrived within the hour. He did a quick evaluation and then gently advised us to gather the rest of the family, as he felt she probably didn't have much longer. I went completely numb as the meaning of those words sank in. I glanced over at my father, who had turned white as a ghost and quickly got him a chair. I realized I had to be strong now, whether I felt it or not.

After making sure Dad was going to be okay, I quietly stepped into the hallway and dialed Shawn's number. When he came to the phone, I carefully explained what was happening and advised him to come as soon as possible. His response left me feeling completely baffled! He told me he had the sniffles and wasn't sure he could make it. For a moment, I thought that maybe he hadn't understood the seriousness of the situation, so I explained again that our mother didn't have much time left. He said he would think about it and hung up. Even though I was surprised at my brother's response, I couldn't allow myself to get upset about it now. I had more important things to deal with!

Throughout the day, I continued to make phone calls to close family members as well as both of my children. By that afternoon, my mother was in a deep sleep and could no longer be wakened. Emotionally and physically exhausted, I sat down in a chair next to her and just marveled at the peaceful look on her face. It was almost as if she knew her battle was almost over. I wondered if she was scared, or if she could even think at all. I looked over at my father, and he looked as though he were in shock.

I suggested that we go outside and get some fresh air, and he wearily agreed. As we walked outside through the front entrance of the building, my father suddenly looked up and said, "I think that is Shawn walking toward us." I looked in the direction he was pointing, and sure enough, it was my brother. I felt relieved for both of my parents' sake, but I still wasn't sure I was willing to give him the benefit of the doubt.

When we returned to my mother's room, I noticed the nursing staff had kindly left a tray of food and coffee for the long hours ahead. As I was helping my dad get settled with his sandwich and coffee, I noticed how ill at ease my brother appeared. Every time I reached out to him, he seemed nervous and withdrawn. I suddenly realized what it took for him to come here. I considered the fact that he was fighting a battle that I knew nothing about. Although my first thought was that he was simply being insensitive, I realized then how much deeper his actions went. As much as we were all hurting, we each handled our pain in different ways. I believed at that moment my brother was doing the best that he could, even if it meant removing himself from the situation he feared the most. As much as I needed him to be fully present, I decided to accept the fact that he was here and somehow get through this together as a family.

It was getting late in the day, and we were all exhausted. Shawn left first, and I promised to call him if Mom passed during the night. Dad was tired and needed his rest, especially so soon after recovering from the flu. I decided to pack a bag and stay overnight at my father's apartment since he was only a block away from Elms Village. The nursing staff knew to call me when the end was near.

The next morning, I woke up with a stiff neck and a feeling of dread as I mentally prepared myself for another day. After some coffee and a quick breakfast, we once again headed over to Elms Village to hold a vigil by my mother's bedside. Before entering my mother's room, the nurse on duty gave us a full report indicating that there wasn't much change overnight; she was still very much with us. It was Sunday morning, and family members came and went. That afternoon, Eric, the hospice chaplain, stopped by. After saying a prayer for my mother, we discreetly met in the hallway and discussed funeral plans. I had asked him earlier to officiate at my mother's funeral, and he had generously agreed. Considering how many of our family members lived out of state and wouldn't be able to make it to the funeral, we decided to keep it very simple with a private service.

As another day came to an end, I was becoming restless. It was inevitable that my mother would pass away soon, but I was starting to wonder if something was holding her back. Was she waiting for something or someone? I decided to take a walk down the hallway and clear my head. As I neared the nurses' station, one of the nurses recognized me and stopped to talk. She told me how sorry she was and shared the details of my mother's last night at dinner in the dining room. Even though speaking had become very difficult for my mother over the past couple of months, that night, she spoke very clearly. After eating two bowls of her favorite ice cream for dinner, she very proudly announced to everyone at the table that she was going home. The nurse then told me that she seemed very much at peace.

By the time she finished, I had tears in my eyes. As grateful as I was to hear this story, I confided that my mother was still hanging on to life, and I wondered if something could be holding her back. The nurse gently told me that this was something she had seen many times before and that sometimes, our loved ones just need to hear us say that it is okay to leave. She further explained that even though my mother appeared to be in a deep sleep, she could still hear me because the hearing is always the last sense people lose.

I thanked her for everything and headed back down the hallway to my mother's room. It was getting late, and I decided to sleep on my father's couch again that night so I could be close by in case anything happened. Before I left, I remembered the nurse's wise words and told my mother how much I loved her, and that it was okay for her to go if she wanted to. I promised her that I would take care of my dad and Shawn and assured her that she had nothing to worry about.

Feeling awkward, I sat back down beside her and looked at her sleeping features. I held her hand and watched her chest gently move up and down as she took each breath. She seemed so far away from this world already. After everything we had been through, I just couldn't imagine what my life was going to be like without her in it.

CHAPTER 22

Jason Street

That night I slept fitfully before finally falling into a deep slumber. By 4:00 a.m. I was wide awake. Suddenly I knew what was holding my mother back! I thought about everything that was important to her and all the things that she needed to hear before she left this world.

After quickly getting dressed, I found the silver cross necklace that I had meant to return. I remembered the comfort and peace it always gave my mother. I carefully put it in my pocket and tiptoed out the front door into the chilly morning air. As I drove the short distance to where my mother hovered between life and death, I could feel my instincts were clearly guiding me.

I parked my car and headed straight for the front entrance of the building. I looked up at the dark sky and noticed that some of the stars had already begun to disappear. I walked soundlessly down the quiet hallway, passing dark rooms where most of the residents were still asleep. When I got to my mother's room, it was dark except for a dim light that filtered through the window, casting a luminous glow over the bed. As my eyes adjusted, I could see my mother's face, and her still figure beneath the blanket. Even though she appeared to be sleeping, I had the feeling that she had been waiting for me.

I sat down in the chair next to her bed and told her that I had a surprise for her. I gently placed the cross necklace around her neck and reminded her of the Mother's Day I had given it to her as a gift. Even though I knew it would be a one-sided conversation, I was very much aware of how important my words were now. It was all that we had left in this final part of our journey together. I reached for my mother's hand as I quietly spoke to her. The tears flowed freely now as I talked about the dynamics of our mother-daughter relationship, the early years, and how much we had been through together. And despite the fact that we had so many difficulties in our lives, she was always my greatest teacher. As I spoke about forgiveness, I could almost feel the energy in the room shift. Deep down, I knew this was the key to setting us both free.

Our past melted away as the sun began to rise, and daylight brightened the room. I noticed that the expression on my mother's face had softened. I reminded her again that it was okay for her to leave us now. Part of me still worried about her confusion caused by dementia, so I began to tell her about angels and the open door leading to the other side, thinking it would help guide her when she left this world.

As I thought of all this, it occurred to me that maybe she was waiting for someone to help guide her home. I suddenly thought of Jason, and it seemed perfectly natural to me. I gently explained that her son Jason was waiting for her, and it was his turn now to be with his mother. I promised her that I would take care of our family, and Shawn and I would be okay.

All of a sudden, her expression changed! She lifted her arms as if reaching out to someone and appeared almost to raise herself off the bed. Startled by the sudden change in my mother, I jumped back and quickly summoned the nurse. I explained what had just happened, and after checking my mother, the nurse assured me that everything was fine. When she left the room, I burst into tears. I thought maybe I had made a mistake, and my emotions had gotten the best of me. But one thing was very clear. My mother could most definitely hear me!

A few minutes later, Cory came into the room, followed by my dad and Shawn. My father brought along a small DVD player so that we could play her favorite music throughout the day. I decided to take a much-needed break and get some coffee and fresh air. After filling my cup with strong coffee and cream, I walked outside into the bright sunshine. I had never felt so physically and emotionally exhausted in all my life. I began to wonder if I had done the right thing after all, by coming here this morning. Maybe it was all just too much for my mother, and somehow, I had managed to make matters worse instead of better. I looked up at the bright blue sky and prayed that she could finally be free of her pain and suffering and leave this world in peace. Then I decided to ask for a sign once my mother had passed so I would know that she made it okay.

I finished my coffee and went back inside to be with the rest of my family. People came and went throughout the day, but my mother remained in a deep slumber. By the time evening rolled around, I was beyond exhausted. Everyone urged me to go home and sleep in my own bed that night, and it didn't take long for me to agree. I whispered goodbye to my mother and lightly kissed her on the forehead. Before leaving, I turned around in the doorway, paused for a moment, and took one last look at her.

When I got home, I was so exhausted that I had to force myself to eat something. My eyelids grew heavy as I slowly climbed the stairs to my bedroom. I decided to take a warm bath and climb into bed. I struggled to close my eyes and kept looking at the clock as if I were waiting for something. I must have dozed off for a short time because I had a very strange dream about my mother that night. I dreamed that we were both standing in my kitchen, and she suddenly began running to the front door. I tried to follow her, but I couldn't seem to keep up. By the time I reached the door, it was wide open, and there was a bright light coming from the other side. Somewhere in the distance, I could hear my phone ringing, and I almost fell out of bed as I scrambled to answer it.

Even before I heard the nurse's voice on the other end, I knew that my mother was gone. She gently reassured me that my mother had passed peacefully in her sleep, and there was no pain or suffering. After I hung up, I looked at the clock and was surprised to see that it was just after 1:00 in the morning. The last time I remembered looking at the clock, it was 12:45 a.m. I couldn't help but think how odd it was, to have such a vivid dream so soon after falling asleep. A few minutes later, I pulled myself together and made the dreaded calls to my father and brother to let them know the sad news of my mother's passing.

After I hung up, I made myself a cup of tea and tried to absorb everything that had happened that last week. I kept thinking that no matter how prepared you are for someone's death; it's going to hurt in the end anyway. Even though I had already been losing her in stages, nothing could have prepared me for this.

I wondered where she was now. I recalled a profound experience that I had long ago after being involved in a very serious car accident. On the way to the hospital in an ambulance, my blood pressure suddenly dropped dangerously low. I felt myself leave this world and enter a place that still leaves me with a sense of peace and pure love. It has strongly influenced my views about what happens to us when we die. I climbed back into bed and closed my eyes, but sleep eluded me once again.

The next morning as I woke up, my mother's death hit me like a ton of bricks. Randy offered to stay home from work to help me with arrangements, but I assured him that I would be fine. After he left, I went on autopilot and made all the necessary phone calls to friends and family. Next, I called Elms Village to find out the location of the funeral home where my mother's body was taken. I could hardly believe my ears when they told me that she was taken to the location on *Jason* Street!

After I hung up, I sat down and began to sob. Horrible, gut-wrenching sobs! All the emotions that I had kept bottled up for so long, finally came spilling out. I must have sat like that for several hours because when I finally calmed down, it was early afternoon. I thought about my prayer just the other day, asking for a sign that my mother was okay after she passed. My dream about the open door, and now the fact that she had arrived at Jason Street, both seemed like the sign I had so desperately prayed for. To a newly bereaved person, it could certainly seem like a divine answer, although I could also understand that some might call it a coincidence. But I, for one, do not believe in coincidences!

Feeling a little better, I called my father to check on him and decided to go over to Elms Village to clear out my mother's room. I donated all her beautiful clothes to the other residents, as I felt this was something my mother would have wanted. When we finished, I looked around the empty room, and it felt strange to see her empty bed and chair, knowing that she was gone now. I thought back to the first day we brought her there. I suddenly realized it would have been exactly two years to the day! We brought my mother to Elms Village on March first, two years earlier and it just so happened to be Leap day, February 29th.

After we finished loading the last of my mother's belongings into the trunk of my car, I made one last trip to the nurses' station. Saying goodbye to the nursing home staff and residents who had become very near and dear to me over the past two years was much harder than I anticipated. In the coming months, I would miss these people with their incredible kindness and support. Before we left, I saw Nancy heading down the hall toward me. With a trembling smile, she hugged me for the very last time. She handed me an envelope with my mother's valuables, which included the silver cross necklace.

When we got back to my dad's apartment, we packed all my mother's remaining items into my dad's storage closet and decided to call it a day. That evening I was restless and rather than giving in to pure exhaustion, I felt the need to keep myself busy. I sifted through the day's mail and noticed that just about every envelope contained something with the word "mom" or "mother" on it. But it didn't stop there. Later I went upstairs to check my emails, and the same thing happened. When I turned on the television before going to bed that night, every other commercial or program seemed to have a theme about mothers. As strange as it all seemed, I decided to keep things in perspective and try to get through the next few days leading up to the funeral, although it was a comforting thought that maybe this *was* God's way of answering my prayer with yet another reassuring sign!

The following afternoon, I got an unexpected phone call from Dad. He tearfully explained that he had decided to walk to the nearby department store to purchase a new shirt for my mother's funeral. As he walked through the store aisles, he suddenly began noticing married couples everywhere and thought back to the times when Mom used to help him pick out his clothes. He realized that he would never have that experience again, and it suddenly hit him that he was alone now.

Sounding flustered and more than a little embarrassed, he admitted that he had some kind of panic attack and couldn't bring himself to continue shopping. Feeling overwhelmed, he quickly left the store without purchasing a shirt. My heart ached as I listened to his sad experience, and I realized that I would have to pay closer attention to my dad now.

The next day was cold and drizzly, and we all met at the funeral home to make the arrangements. My mother was going to be buried at the Veterans Cemetery, and we decided to have the inscription *Gone Home* on her headstone, in reference to her last words at the dinner table that night when she proudly announced that she was going home. I brought in her favorite blue dress to be buried in and chose a wreath of daisies for the casket, which was her favorite flower. I also agreed to read the eulogy that I had carefully written for my mother.

Everything was planned right down to the last detail, which included the Scottish bagpipes that my father insisted on, honoring our Scottish heritage. With nothing left to do for the next couple of days leading up to the funeral, I started to feel anxious. The more I tried to relax, the worse I felt. I realized then that I had only been going through the motions. Keeping busy was just a diversion to keep myself from completely falling apart.

Over the next several days, I somehow managed to keep an eye on Dad as I tried to adjust to my mother's death and my own raging emotions. Once again, I was thankful for the support of my new friends. Many of them had also lost loved ones and expressed their condolences. After they shared their experiences, it was clear to me they understood the emptiness one feels after caring for a loved one.

The day of the funeral was sunny and unusually warm for early March. We all met at the funeral home on Jason Street, and I was again reminded of the strange circumstances behind the street's name. Out of all six locations, my mother ended up at the one with the same name as my late brother. I couldn't deny the strong connection I felt. It gave me goosebumps!

Moments after arriving at the funeral home, the director came out and asked my father and me if we would like to make sure everything was in order before proceeding with the funeral. I handed him the silver cross necklace that had once brought my mother so much comfort and requested that she be buried with it. It was the last act of love I could do for her.

As I moved towards the blue casket, my legs turned to rubber. I held my breath as I peered inside and was overcome by a wave of grief that felt strangely familiar to me. Seeing my mother's lifeless body came as such a shock, even though I had thought about this moment for months. I tried to take comfort in the fact that my mother's spirit was free now, and there would be no more suffering and pain.

My thoughts were suddenly interrupted by the sounds of my grandchildren clamoring into the room. I turned around and quickly plastered a smile on my face. I was determined not to let them see me cry. The funeral was simple yet meaningful, and afterward, we all drove to the cemetery for the burial service.

After the last prayer was read, I stood and carefully placed my hand on the coffin before slowly walking away. I left with an odd sense of completion, and sadness washed over me. It was all over now. There was nothing left to do but let the dust settle. Feeling dazed, we headed home.

The next morning, I woke up feeling tired and edgy. At first, I was grateful for the peace and solitude after Randy left for work, but soon the silence became deafening. As I made my way downstairs, rancid thoughts filled my head, and the air felt too heavy to breathe. I felt betrayed as I thought of how hard I struggled to forgive and understand my mother. Now the past several years suddenly had less meaning and felt more like a cruel joke. How was it possible to feel so much pain after all we had just been through? What good was it now?

I was completely overwhelmed! I went into a frenzy, putting everything away that reminded me of my mother. I scrubbed and cleaned and threw away all the plants and flowers from the funeral that were sitting on my table. I couldn't stand to see one more thing that would eventually wither and die.

I realized I probably wasn't acting very rational, but then again, I wasn't feeling rational. Suddenly I was nine years old again. I began to remember how I felt growing up when my mother would pack her bags and leave, only this time, it was for good, and my mother was never coming back! I was feeling more like an abandoned child than a grown adult.

Throughout my life, my mother had abandoned me in every possible way: physically, emotionally, and now with her death. After her illness, when I made the decision to care for my parents, I understood the huge risk involved. I set aside my feelings of resentment and mistrust. I took a leap of faith. Even though the stakes were high, I was willing to give my mother another chance. I never stopped longing for her, never gave up on the possibility that she would someday love me.

Now that things had changed between us, now that so much was healed, I would have to accept my loss and learn to live without her all over again. No matter how hard I tried, I couldn't shake the unexpected flood of emotions and memories. As the days turned into weeks, and eventually into months, I braced myself for the intensifying storm.

CHAPTER 23

Picking up the pieces

To say, I struggled with my mother's death would have been an understatement. It was an especially confusing time because I both loved and hated her all at the same time. It took four long years after her death to feel comfortable putting up a framed photograph of my mother in the house. Losing a parent is hard for anybody, but if the relationship was troubled, I believe it can actually prolong the grieving process because there is so much more work and healing to be done.

Not long after my mother's death, I started dreaming of her. She always appeared radiant and much younger, and I looked forward to these dreams. One day, I realized that I could love her more freely now than I ever could when she was alive.

My mother's death was the beginning of an end of something I carried deep within me for as long as I can remember. Picking up the pieces after she was gone was harder than I ever could have imagined. It was my strong will and determination to heal that eventually led me back to a place I once called home, to soothe the deep scars that still lingered.

My mother had always been a mystery to me. Deep down, I knew that discovering the secrets to her past held the key to finding peace and understanding. It was important for me to find out more about the person she once was.

About a year after my mother died, my search took me back to where it all began. Late that spring, Cory, my father, and I decided to take a trip back to North Dakota. We would be visiting many family members along the way from both my father's and mother's side of the family. It would prove to be very interesting, especially since I hadn't seen many of them in years! Our trip was going to be for only five days, so we had to make the most of the time we had.

Our first visit was with my dad's oldest brother, Keith, and his wife, Bethany. My aunt Bethany happened to be my mother's best friend before she married my father. It is, in fact, how my parents met. Yes, this does get confusing at times! My father enjoyed visiting with his brother, and they obviously had a lot of catching up to do. It gave me the perfect opportunity to talk to Aunt Bethany and find out what my mother was like before she met and married my father. My aunt was happy to help, and she carefully described my mother as being quiet, shy, and somewhat lacking in self-confidence.

My mother was fresh out of beauty school when they met. Aunt Bethany managed a beauty shop and hired her for a position that had just opened up. It didn't take long for them to become fast friends. My aunt later introduced my mother to her brother-in-law (my father) at a picnic, and the rest, as they say, was history!

We also talked about more personal things, and I learned about the fateful day my brother Jason passed away. This was something my mother was never able to talk about. According to my aunt, it was Christmas of 1961, and everyone from my father's side of the family was visiting at my grandparents' farm.

My mother had a bad cold, and her doctor had prescribed penicillin. Just a few days after Christmas, on December 28th, my mother began having terrible pain and thought she was going into labor. She wasn't due for several more weeks, and my father drove her to the nearest hospital, which was nearly thirty miles away. Aunt Bethany and Uncle Keith decided to ride with them.

When they got to the hospital, my mother was in excruciating pain, and they took her straight into the delivery room. A little while later, my father was told he had a son, but he didn't survive. My mother was resting in a room down the hall, and he was permitted to visit her while my aunt and uncle remained in the waiting area. The visit was brief; however, as my mother said she didn't feel much like talking.

A short time later, my father decided to go back to my grandparents' farm to pick up a change of clothing for my mother while Bethany stayed with her. After my father left, she poured out all of the sad details to her closest friend. The doctor believed that my mother had some sort of an allergic reaction to the penicillin, which had caused her to go into labor. She was able to hold her precious son in her arms while he took his last breath and quietly passed away. He was wrapped in a blanket, and the nurse gently took him from her. It was the first and last time my mother ever saw him.

Later she confessed that she felt guilty for taking the medicine and was convinced that she was responsible for her child's death. She said she felt like a failure as both a mother and a wife. Aunt Bethany believed that she never really recovered from this. She thought that she suffered some kind of depression as a result.

My grandparents were beside themselves when they learned the sad news and offered a family plot in the cemetery not far from their farm. They took care of all the arrangements and chose a small white casket and a headstone with a little lamb bearing his name. My mother seemed to be in shock and barely made it through that day.

I was overcome with sadness as I listened to the tragic story. I imagined my mother all those years ago, consumed by guilt and grief for her child. It was the first of many stories that I would hear on this trip as I delved deeper into my mother's past.

By the time we were ready to leave the next day, I had learned so much about my mother that I already felt I knew her on a much more personal level. Our journey continued to Bismarck, the city where I grew up.

After checking in to our hotel, we decided to take a drive past the house where we lived until I was eleven years old. Not much had changed except for the house that now occupied the large empty lot where I once loved to play. I pulled over to the curb and just sat for a moment, gazing at the house that still held so many memories. It amazed me at how those memories, both good and bad, could still have such a powerful effect on me.

I remembered the layout of the house. In my mind's eye, I could still see my childhood bedroom, with the cotton-candy-pink walls and ruffled curtains. I imagined myself as a young girl, riding my bike through the neighborhood on an afternoon just like this one. As I rolled down the window, I could hear the drone of a lawnmower and someone's radio playing a familiar song.

I was surprised to see that little had changed in the quiet cul-de-sac where I once lived. The traditional ranch and split-level homes with shuttered windows, manicured lawns, and carefully tended flowerbeds still looked much the same as I remembered. I pictured myself running up the steps to the front door, hesitating only for a moment to get a sense of my mother's mood before cautiously entering the house. Something I had learned to do at a very early age.

I quickly shook off the memory and decided to drive past the elementary school that I used to attend. Just being here in my old neighborhood dredged up so many long-ago memories, and it seemed as though I could feel my mother everywhere. Rather than feeling nostalgic, I was starting to feel a bit overwhelmed as past and present became one. I was overcome by intense emotion and felt strangely vulnerable. I had to fight back a sudden urge to escape. I decided I had had enough for one day. It was time to head back to the hotel room.

My dad and Cory seemed to be enjoying our trip down memory lane. And I certainly couldn't deny that it was nice to get away! But I was on a mission. I knew that coming here would not only help me find closure; facing the past was necessary to understand the present.

The next morning, we were on the road again. We decided to visit the cemetery where my late brother Jason was buried and pay our respects to several other family members as well, including my beloved paternal grandparents. Standing before my brother's grave, I solemnly bowed my head and could almost sense that he and my mother were together again.

I thought about the story I had recently heard and felt a new sense of sorrow. Not just for my mother but for all of us and the life we might have had, free from the shadow of grief. I remembered coming here as a child and placing flowers on his headstone as my mother looked on. Deep down I sometimes envied Jason, especially when I noticed the look of love and tenderness on my mother's face. I always wished she would look at me like that. I wondered if they could somehow look down and see us standing here now?

When we left the cemetery, the sky looked dark and threatening, and the wind had started to pick up. As we drove through the pouring rain, my dad mentioned that the town where he and my mother were married was only a short distance away. The rain finally let up as we drove through the small-town streets of Ellendale.

Just as the sun was coming out, we spotted the beautiful old church at the other end of town, and I pulled the car over to take some pictures. I stood there for a moment imagining my mother as a young and beautiful bride, blissful and in love, basking in the glow of anticipation. I glanced over at my father, and I could tell that he was remembering.

Since we were in the general area, I wanted to visit my grandparents' farm, where I had so many fond memories as a child. As I continued to drive in that direction, the pavement petered out, and we soon came upon a rutted gravel road that led to the abandoned farm. We passed by the fields where I used to run and play, and soon, the familiar house came into view. I pulled into the muddy yard and immediately noticed that my grandmother's beautiful flower garden was now overrun by weeds and tall grass. As I took it all in, I was pleasantly surprised to see that the lilac trees were in full bloom.

Even though the house sat dark and deserted, I imagined the warm cozy kitchen that once held the delectable aromas of brewed coffee, freshly baked bread and roasted chicken dinners. I could still hear my grandfather's deep, gentle voice calling me Suzie. Something about the way he said my pet name always made me feel warm and special. I would often dream of coming back to this house to stay. But the dream eventually faded, and there was emptiness.

After reminiscing with my father about the place we both knew and loved, I pulled back onto the gravel road once again. The farm, the hills, and fields, were all etched in my memory. I once had roots here, a place where I belonged, and I felt comforted.

Our next stop was Akrin, the little town where my mother grew up. Several of her siblings and other family members still lived there, and my aunt Ginny was expecting us that afternoon for a family get-together.

When we arrived, the sky was dark and gloomy. I thought it made the town look rather depressing as we drove down the almost deserted main street. We checked into our hotel, and since it was still a little early, we took a drive around the neighborhood until we reached the house where my mother grew up. It was an older, single-story house with large shuttered windows and a long, hedge-lined walkway that led to the front door.

I noticed that the new owners had given it a fresh coat of paint, and the yard was neat and well kept. As I observed the house from across the street, I was reminded of how incredibly small it was. It was especially shocking when I considered the fact that my mother came from a large family with nine people!

That evening, we drove out to my mother's oldest sister's home for dinner. It had started to rain again, and I felt a little uneasy when I spotted the house in the distance. When we arrived, we were welcomed by an assortment of cousins, aunts, and uncles. I hadn't seen most of these people in the almost thirty years since my wedding day. It was a little overwhelming.

Even though most of these people were all but strangers to me, we managed to bridge the gap of years and quickly got re-acquainted. After dinner, I was in the kitchen helping with the dishes when I started a conversation with both of my mother's sisters. I was somewhat shocked and taken aback when they began making negative comments about my mother. I found it rude and disrespectful since she had only passed away a year earlier.

Both of my aunts complained that my late grandfather had always favored my mother when they were children. They obviously still had hard feelings about it. My mother was the third oldest of seven children and the second oldest daughter. I had always heard that my mother was her father's favorite, especially because she looked very much like him, with the same ice-blue eyes. Since he was an alcoholic, his moods were quick to change, often revealing his darker side that suggested an abusive nature.

I found it rather disturbing that there still seemed to be some kind of sibling rivalry between the sisters, even after all this time. For some reason, I was under the impression that they had always been somewhat close, but now I understood that closeness was part of a love-hate relationship.

After the kitchen was cleaned up and the dishes were put away, I noticed that my aunts were not being very nice to each other. They were bickering amongst themselves, and soon their voices grew louder. It made me feel uncomfortable, and I decided then that this was all part of being in a dysfunctional family. I didn't want anything more to do with it, and soon after, we said our goodbyes and left.

We drove back to the depressing little town where my mother spent most of her young life and decided to call it a night. Even the hotel we stayed in was old and dilapidated. After a hot shower, I climbed into bed and snuggled under the covers. I soon fell into a deep and troubled sleep. I dreamt about my mother being trapped in a tiny house, full of angry, miserable people in a sad little town. I woke up with a start and realized my dream was most likely not far from the truth. The more I thought about it, the more I understood my mother.

CHAPTER 24

Putting the pieces together

The next morning the sun was shining bright, and we were all eager to be on the road again. On the way back home, my father wanted to go through Nebraska, to visit the assisted living community where my parents lived before coming to Colorado. We decided it would be a good place to stop for the night.

Since it was a good eight-hour drive, I decided to ask my dad to tell me more about the early years of their marriage. As the story unfolded, I could see my young parents starting a new life together in a small town. In truth, it was an Indian reservation. My dad's first job was working for the Bureau of Indian Affairs, and they lived in a house just outside of the reservation in New Town, North Dakota. My mother was a new bride and anxious to become a good wife as they settled into married life.

While my dad progressed with his new job, my mother found herself isolated and alone in a small town where she was very much a minority. The population consisted mostly of Native Americans, whose culture and background was very different from my mother's. I don't know what she thought of them, but I imagine they weren't very interested in her. She spent most of her time alone, learning how to cook, trying out new recipes, and being a good housewife. But soon she became bored, lonely, and restless. She was young and strong and eager, with no outlet for her energy or emotions. When she discovered she was pregnant with her first child, she was suddenly filled with hope and looked forward to being a good mother. I imagined how she must have felt as I remembered being pregnant with my first child. It was a time of joy and excitement.

After the loss of her child, she sank into a deep depression. She blamed herself and lost her confidence as both a mother and wife. She was far away from family and friends, with no one to talk with. My dad sadly admitted that he did not feel comfortable talking with her about her feelings.

He was a man of his time, raised to be strong and unyielding. Emotions were something he typically shied away from. To make matters worse, her father passed away not long after. Her grief and unhappiness became almost unbearable, as the feelings of isolation and loneliness soon took over. Deep down, my dad believed that she blamed him, mainly because he was not there for her, either emotionally or physically. He said he did his best to try and make her happy by being successful and a good provider.

My mother soon discovered that she was pregnant once again. This time, she was not as happy with the idea as she was the first time. Her grief was still too fresh with the loss of both her father and son, all within the same year. Her fear became her worst enemy as she imagined failing again as a mother.

On a warm summer day in July, I came into the world. My birth was anything but easy, and to make matters worse, I was born in the breech position, which means bottom first. I was delivered by C-section, and both my parents were terrified at the prospect of losing another child, but God had other plans.

From the time my parents brought me home from the hospital, my mother became a nervous wreck and panicked about every little thing. My father suggested that maybe she could use some help, and my mother's youngest sister Emily agreed to come and stay for a while.

Things soon settled down, and life became more routine. My mother was just beginning to feel more comfortable with her new role when my dad announced that they were moving again. My dad's job with the Bureau of Indian Affairs took them to another small-town reservation, and they packed up once again and moved to Rosebud, South Dakota.

My parents soon realized that it was going to be the same dire situation again, only this time it was in a town that was even further away from family and friends. My mother once again became isolated and lonely, and it eventually took its toll on their marriage, causing growing resentment. My father soon got a new job with the state water commission, and my mother was thrilled when she learned that they would be moving to the city of Bismarck, North Dakota.

They packed up once again and rented a house close to my dad's new office. Even though it was a big improvement, things were far from perfect. My mother started seeing more of her family again, which included her mother and most of her siblings. Many of them still lived in the same small town where they were born and raised. My mother's oldest sister, Ginny, married a farmer, and the others had menial jobs. They seemed to accept their lives for what they were and never strived for more. They sometimes acted jealous of my parents and would jokingly refer to my father as a "good catch."

They would fight and argue, and my mother would get angry and stay in a bad mood that lasted for days, and sometimes weeks. I always felt nervous when my mother's family came to visit. When they arrived, everyone seemed happy at first. They would laugh and joke amongst themselves, and everyone would smile at me. Before long beer and alcohol were served, and voices got louder and angrier. It used to scare me, and I always wondered what made them so mad.

Eventually, my dad advanced to a better position. He got a promotion and worked for the state highway department as a civil engineer. He designed bridges and did consultations all over the state, as well as neighboring areas. Since he was making a better salary, he decided it was time to put down roots and buy a house.

My mother was happy to have a permanent place to live finally and loved the idea of looking at new homes. When they bought their new house, my mother wanted to go all out and buy new furniture and home décor. They soon began entertaining and invited family and friends over to see the new house.

A short time later, my aunt Emily moved in and stayed in the basement while she was between jobs. My mother soon grew tired of my aunt's wild and vivacious ways, and her sometimes overly flirtatious nature. Emily eventually moved out, but the rest of the family continued to visit, especially on the weekends.

I can still recall my mother telling me to go outside and play when things would grow tense and voices escalated. There seemed to be family secrets that made my mother uncomfortable, and she did her best to keep them from me. The more my mother's family came to visit, the worse the fights got.

They eventually stopped speaking to each other, and things quieted down for a while. But my mother's moods grew worse. My father's job required more and more of his time as he continued to work hard at his career. My mother spent more time alone, and her anger and depression became all-consuming.

She missed her job as a beautician and toyed with the idea of going back to work. But my father had strong opinions. He insisted that he made enough money. He made it clear that he preferred his wife to stay at home and raise a family. My father had very old-fashioned ideas about women working outside the home, and my mother did not want to disappoint him. She was destined to follow in her mother's footsteps, if not for the lack of confidence she felt, but because she had no other role model.

As I listened to the story of my parents' early years, I could only guess what my mother's life was like as a young wife and mother. My father had grown wiser over the years, and I easily sensed some of his regrets.

I thought about how she struggled to fit into a world where she felt she didn't belong, all while facing social isolation and grieving the loss of her child and father. I imagined how frightened and alone she must have felt, with no real support of any kind. She was haunted by a physically and emotionally abusive childhood that left lifelong scars while still trying to deal with her dysfunctional family as an adult.

Suddenly I felt nothing but love and deep compassion for my mother as I mentally stepped inside her shoes. There was so much to think about and consider. I tried to put all the pieces together. The hours on the road flew by as I took in my father's story. We suddenly fell silent, lost in our thoughts, and my father looked humbled. We were getting close to our destination and looked forward to grabbing a quick dinner and getting a good night's rest.

The next morning, we drove through the town of Scottsbluff; everything looked the same as it did the day we left. We were all very quiet as we drove up the long driveway to the assisted living facility where my parents had lived just a few years earlier. I remembered how uncertain the future was as we drove away that morning not so long ago.

It seemed odd walking through the front lobby, which still felt so familiar. I gazed up at the second floor where my parents' old apartment used to be, and it made me sad, knowing that they no longer lived there. My dad seemed pleased that several of the residents still remembered us. Most had heard about my mother's passing and stopped to express their condolences.

One of the maintenance men who still remembered my dad asked if we would like to see the old apartment again since it was vacant at the moment. We both eagerly agreed as we followed him up the stairs to the second floor. When he opened the door, he told us to take our time and left us alone with our memories. After he left, we just stood there in silence remembering the last time we were there.

I glanced at the corner where my mother's rocking chair used to be, and I could still see her, rocking away without a care in the world. It was hard to imagine that just three years earlier; life was so different. I took several more pictures before we left. It was time to head back home again.

We arrived home just in time for Father's Day weekend. I had quite a collection of pictures from our trip and decided to make them into a memory book for my dad to enjoy. I will remember this trip for as long as I live. I learned so many things about my mother, and I decided to write them all down in a journal.

In the days that followed, I thought many times of my mother and all that I knew about her now. It was like fitting pieces of a puzzle together and seeing the whole picture for the first time. It certainly gave me a new perspective of where we came from, and how the family dynamic was created. I was beginning to understand that my mother was just as much a victim as I was—although I prefer to think of us as survivors. Could I have withstood that many years of loneliness and grief? I had, of course, in my own way.

When I thought about my marriage, I felt relief that Randy and I had somehow managed not to lose our sense of self in order to please the other. Over the years, we had our share of challenges to overcome, but I believe it was our love and respect for each other that gave us the courage to persevere. I was starting to realize where my inner strength came from.

I have learned to accept the legacy of my past as I embrace the present and look forward to the future. I will always consider my mother as my greatest teacher as I continue on this journey. As I end this story, my biggest wish is that it brings faith, hope, and inspiration to all who read it!

EPILOGUE

Moving forward

I am still a work in progress. As I worked through the grief of my mother's passing, my pain became the inspiration to write this book. From this deeply personal place, I have learned some of life's most valuable lessons: acceptance, compassion, and forgiveness, just to name a few. But most importantly, this journey has given me an unshakeable faith in God and what lies beyond this human life. They say you can't choose your family, and it's probably a good thing because I know without a doubt, I would never have knowingly chosen mine. But I do believe that God chose them for me, and I consider it a blessing every single day of my life!

For much of my life, I believed what my mother told me as a child—that I was not really her daughter. Choosing to believe this made it possible to hang on to the hope that there was still someone out there who would claim me and love me unconditionally. I understand now how much a daughter needs her mother. It is a primal bond that can never be broken.

I was always determined to become the person I always thought I could be, by looking deep within and breaking the chains that weighed so heavily upon my heart. It took years of understanding not only myself but the woman who was my mother. It was necessary to learn about her past and what made her who she was. The more I searched, the more I learned. And the more I discovered, the more I realized I could finally decode the pieces of my past that so desperately needed healing. The wounds we inherit from our parents are the hardest to heal.

I will always remember a conversation I had with my father long ago. After a particularly devastating fight with my mother, I asked, "Why do I always have to be the strong one?" He simply replied, "Because you are the strong one." I never forgot those wise words, and they became my mantra many times throughout my life.

I am grateful for the life I have lived, and even more so for the relationships I have with my own children and my three grandchildren. I love the closeness we all share and the new history we are weaving into the fabric of this family. I have come to believe that every person and life experience has something important to teach us if we choose to see it.

As I went through the process of understanding my mother, the world around me softened, and I felt compassion for others as I never have before. As I think about the people in my life, I have learned to look a little deeper and consider the fact that there are many sources behind the scenes that are responsible for their beliefs and behavior.

After my father-in-law passed away, I was again reminded of another part of my past that was quite painful. Even though at the end of his life, he admitted that he still could not accept me, I chose to forgive him anyway. No matter how much people hurt you, it helps to remember that it comes from a place rooted deep inside of them that may not be a reflection of you. Ultimately, it becomes our responsibility to choose what we do with it.

As I continue to care for my father, I am amazed at what I learn from him and how he has influenced my life. My brother still chooses not to be a part of the caregiving process, and I have learned to accept it and live my life in peace.

I have come to realize that it takes an enormous amount of energy to be angry. It occupies a lot of space in our thoughts. I believe that the longer we carry this negative energy around with us, the more damage it does to our bodies and minds.

When a loved one suffers from mental health issues, it affects the entire family and can be devastating. Although my mother was never formally diagnosed with a specific mental illness, we do have our theories. In the 1960s and 1970s, mental disorders were subject to prejudice and stigmatization in society, and people were often judged and misunderstood.

There weren't as many treatment options available back then as there are now, and people like my mother usually suffered in silence. This led to shame, anger, and a feeling of being different from everyone else, an outcast. No matter how people try to hide such feelings, they affect every aspect of their lives.

It is sometimes difficult to understand exactly what a mental illness is, but it is important to know that the sufferer usually craves relief from their inner turmoil—often more than anything else—and deserves support and understanding. Dealing with a family member who has depression, bipolar disorder, anxiety, or substance abuse can tear families apart and have long-lasting effects as it did in my own family.

One of the most important things I have learned through my experience is that educating yourself about your loved one's mental illness is just as important as with any other kind of illness. In hindsight, I can honestly say now that my biggest regret comes from my own personal estrangement from my mother. I know this is a complicated issue. While I agree that many situations are capable of being healed and forgiven, I also agree that it is necessary to avoid toxic relationships, especially if you feel threatened. We all must do what is best for ourselves as well as other loved ones.

I have since learned that an estimated one in five people has some sort of mental illness in any given year. It can be temporary or long-lasting and begin at any age. There are many things that can cause mental illness, such as genetic or environmental factors. Risk factors include traumatic experiences, on-going stress, brain damage, inherited traits, among others.

As I grew older, especially after my children were born, I worried that I would turn out like my mother. I was always aware of the impact of my childhood and how it might affect my relationships with my children. Although I still sometimes suffered from anxiety, which reared its ugly head during certain situations, I decided to seek professional therapy to help me be a better parent.

I was in my late twenties, and my children were still very young when I decided to continue the therapy I had started in my teens. It quite literally saved my life. There is never any shame in asking for help; in fact, it is the responsible thing to do. I will always be thankful that I made that decision long ago. I didn't heal overnight, and it was a long and sometimes brutal process that lasted long after my sessions were over.

I believe that this is what saved me and helped me be a loving daughter when my parents needed me the most. I will always be grateful for this life experience with my parents, as it helped me complete the healing process I began earlier and allowed me to close a huge void in my life. I am able to look back now and feel compassion not just for my family, but for others as well. My heart is full!

APPENDIX A

Parkinson's disease

What exactly is Parkinson's disease? Simply put, Parkinson's disease is a movement disorder that affects the central nervous system. It occurs when nerve cells that create and use a brain chemical called dopamine either stop working or die. Dopamine coordinates movement and sends messages to the brain. When a malfunction occurs, it can cause tremors, problems with balance and walking, stiffness, and rigidity. It can also cause secondary or non-movement symptoms such as depression, constipation, sleep disorders, cognitive and psychiatric symptoms.

Since Parkinson's is a progressive disease, symptoms will slowly worsen over time. Each person will have a unique experience living with this disease, and side effects, symptoms, and progression will vary from person to person. One of the most important things that my family and I learned was how important it was to have access to a good healthcare team. These experts should include an occupational therapist, speech and language therapist, social worker, movement disorder specialist, and if possible, a nutritionist and psychologist to help manage these issues. Working with a competent healthcare team is important to the well-being and quality of life for your loved one.

There is no definitive way to diagnose Parkinson's disease. Usually, a neurologist will review your medical history and perform specific tests, such as a blood test, brain scan, or other imaging tests to rule out other possible diseases, then make a determination based on your symptoms.

There is no cure for Parkinson's disease. There are certain medications that can help manage symptoms, but they don't work the same for everyone and must be adjusted to the patient's individual needs. One of the most common medications on the market is Levodopa. It is usually taken in combination with carbidopa to prevent the levodopa from being broken down in the body before it reaches the brain. It is generally only effective for around five years and after that, other medications may be added to help with symptoms.

One thing that I always wondered about is why certain people get Parkinson's disease, while others don't. It was a real concern for me, especially since genetics were involved. Although there are ongoing studies on this subject, I have learned that only 15 percent of people who have the disease have a family history of it. The cause of Parkinson's disease is usually unknown. Some studies show that a genetic mutation can increase your risk of getting the disease, but it does not mean you will inherit it. There is also thought to be a connection between Parkinson's disease and exposure to pesticides and solvents. According to research, a combination of environmental and genetic factors could be responsible for causing Parkinson's.

If you have a loved one or know someone who has Parkinson's disease, the best way to help them is to learn everything you can about the condition. It's important to understand the progressive symptoms, side effects from medications, and treatment options. Life with Parkinson's requires adjustment, and educating yourself will help you face the future as the disease progresses. Make sure you have a good support system. Although having family and friends are always helpful, there are support groups and organizations that offer great resources and can help educate patients and their families. I have listed some of these organizations below.

Helpful Resources:

A Place for Mom
866-518-0936
https://www.aplaceformom.com/planning-and-advice/articles/parkinsons-disease-in-the-elderly

American Parkinson Disease Association
1-800-223-2732
www.apdaparkinson.org

Family Caregiver Alliance
National Center on Caregiving
https://www.caregiver.org/parkinsons-disease-caregiving

National Institute of Neurological Disorders and Stroke
https://www.ninds.nih.gov/Disorders/All-Disorders/Parkinsons-Disease-Information-Page

Parkinson's Foundation
1-800-473-4636
https://www.parkinson.org/about-us

Parkinson's Institute and Clinical Center
www.thepi.org

The Brain Initiative
https://www.braininitiative.nih.gov

The Michael J. Fox Foundation
https://www.michaeljfox.org/foundation/promise.html

WebMD
https://www.webmd.com/parkinsons-disease/guide/parkinsons-caregivers#1

Recommended Reading:

Giroux, Monique L. M.D. *Optimal Health with Parkinson's Disease: A Guide to Integrating Lifestyle, Alternative, and Conventional Medicine.* New York: Demos Medical Publishing, 2015.

Newson, Hal. *HOPE: Four Keys to a Better Quality of Life for Parkinson's People, 2nd Edition.* Washington: Northwest Parkinson's Foundation, 2006.

Okun, Michael S. M.D. *10 Breakthrough Therapies for Parkinson's Disease.* Books4Patients, 2015.

Schwarz, Shelley Peterman. *Parkinson's Disease: 300 Tips for Making Life Easier, 2nd Edition.* New York: Demos Medical Publishing, 2006.

Shifke, Howard. *Fighting Parkinson's…and Winning: A memoir of my recovery from Parkinson's Disease.* South Carolina: CreateSpace Independent Publishing Platform, 2017.

Silver, Robert J. *Keepin' On: Living Well with Parkinson's Disease.* New Mexico: Nighthawk Press, 2018.

Vine, John M. *A Parkinson's Primer: An Indispensable Guide to Parkinson's Disease for Patients and Their Families.* Philadelphia: Paul Dry Books, 2017.

APPENDIX B

What is Lewy body dementia?

If you or someone you know has been diagnosed with Lewy body dementia, you might be wondering what to expect. When my mother was diagnosed with this condition, it came as a surprise. Although many people have never heard of LBD, it is not all that uncommon. According to the National Institute on Aging, LBD affects over 1 million people in the United States alone. Almost half of all people diagnosed with Parkinson's disease will develop some type of Parkinson's dementia. One of the better-known people to be diagnosed with Lewy body dementia was the late Robin Williams.

LBD consists of two different conditions with similar symptoms. One is dementia with Lewy bodies, and the other is Parkinson's dementia. LBD is a type of dementia that is associated with abnormal protein deposits in the brain called Lewy bodies. It affects motor control and thinking. Lewy body dementia can affect how you process information and also have physical symptoms such as tremors and movement difficulties.

As the disease progresses, there can be many unpredictable characteristics. However, progression can vary significantly from one person to another. In the early stages, you might notice distortions of reality that may involve hallucinations, restlessness, and sleep disorders. Although memory is still pretty much intact, there may be mild cognitive issues like confusion and delusions.

In the middle stages, you might notice a significant decline in cognition. The strange thing about this is that it tends to fluctuate almost daily and makes it hard for family and caregivers to understand why there is such a variation between good days and bad. Other symptoms include the inability to control bodily functions. Things can become complicated if your loved one develops incontinence. They may not recognize or understand the need to empty their bladder and react with resistance or combative behavior when you try to assist them. Other complications include increased impairment of motor skills, which can lead to a high risk of falls. It is usually during this time when family must make the difficult decision to choose nursing home placement or outside help.

Because LBD is a progressive disorder, almost all symptoms will worsen over time. In the later stages, speech may become absent or nothing more than a whisper, making communication difficult. There is usually an extreme increase in muscle stiffness and rigidity, and sometimes a sensitivity to touch develops. Because of increased weakness, your loved one may become more susceptible to pneumonia and other types of infection. It is at this stage that care will become necessary for almost all activities of daily living.

Diagnosing Lewy body dementia is difficult because an absolute diagnosis can only be confirmed after death by a post-mortem examination. After other conditions are ruled out, a diagnosis is made primarily based on the person's symptoms that fit the criteria for LBD. There is no cure for this disease, and symptoms are usually managed by medication, which must be monitored and adjusted as needed.

The average lifespan for someone diagnosed with LBD is five to seven years. However, this greatly varies with each individual, especially since diagnosis is not always immediate; in any particular case, the end of life is difficult to predict. No one understands what causes LBD, but I hope that one day we might understand this disease and with continuing medical advancements, there may someday be a cure!

Helpful Resources:

Alzheimer's Speaks
Shifting Our Dementia Care Culture
https://www.alzheimersspeaks.com

Lewy Body Dementia
Learning to Live with Lewy Body Dementia
www.Lewybodydementia.ca/resources-for-lewy-body-dementia

Lewy Body Dementia Association
1-404-975-2322
1-844-311-0587 (toll-free LBD Caregiver Link)
www.lbda.org

Lewy Body Dementia Resource Center
Bringing Awareness, Supporting with Love
516-218-2026
https://lewybodyresourcecenter.org/what-is-lbd

MedlinePlus
National Library of Medicine
www.medlineplus.gov

Michael J. Fox Foundation for Parkinson's Research
1-800-708-7644 (toll-free)
www.michaeljfox.org

National Institute on Aging. "What Is Lewy Body Dementia?"
https://www.nia.nih.gov/health/what-lewy-body-dementia

Parkinson's Foundation
1-800-473-4636 (toll-free)
helpline@parkinson.org
www.parkinson.org

UCSF Memory and Aging Center
Weill Institute for Neurosciences
https://memory.ucsf.edu/lewy-body-dementias

Recommended Reading:

Ashlskog, J. Eric. *Dementia with Lewy Bodies and Parkinson's Disease Dementia: Patient, Family, and Clinician Working Together for Better Outcomes, 1st Edition.* New York: Oxford University Press, 2013.

Beller Health, and Jerry Beller. *Lewy Body Dementia (2019 Edition): Dementia with Lewy Bodies (DLB), Parkinson's Disease Dementia (PDD), (Collections Series).* Independently Published, 2019.

Leatherdale, Lyndsay. *Sundown Dementia, Vascular Dementia and Lewy Body Dementia Explained. Stages, symptoms, signs, prognosis, diagnoses, treatments, progression, care and mood changes are all covered, 1st Edition.* IMB Publishing, 2013.

Mullens, Dr. Jane M. *Finding the Light in Dementia: A Guide for Families, Friends and Caregivers.* Ohio: DUETcare Publishing, 2017.

Smits, Angel. *When Reasoning No Longer Works: A Practical Guide for Caregivers Dealing with Dementia & Alzheimer's Care.* Colorado: Parker Hayden Media, 2017.

Whitworth, Helen Buell, "MS BSN", and James Whitworth. *A Caregiver's Guide to Lewy Body Dementia.* New York: Demos Medical Publishing, 2010.

APPENDIX C
Caregiving

Are you a caregiver? If so, chances are you just fell into this role like most of us do, without any plan or warning. At some point in our lives, many of us will find ourselves caring for a loved one. In fact, according to survey statistics, over sixty-five million people in the United States provide care. As more people are living with chronic illnesses, and the elderly are living longer, this number will only continue to increase.

What exactly is a caregiver? The basic definition of a caregiver is someone who provides care or help to another person in need. The person receiving care may be a parent, spouse, or a child with special needs. Not all caregivers are family members, and some are employed.

Caregiving is not an easy job and requires lots of patience and dedication. It is true what they say: "Caregiving is not for the faint of heart!" Some of the duties performed by caregivers include shopping, cooking, cleaning, providing transportation to and from doctor appointments, and intimate care such as bathing, going to the toilet, or dressing. The list could go on and on. You may be a caregiver and not even realize it!

Most caregivers are on call 24 hours a day, seven days a week. It can become very stressful and draining over time and may take a toll on your own health as a result. Finding time for yourself becomes harder, and you may eventually suffer from caregiver burnout. Caregivers may also face an increased risk of chronic illness, depression, and a decline in quality of life.

If you are new to caregiving, you may feel overwhelmed and not sure just where to begin. Although everyone has a different set of circumstances, one of the most important things I have learned is to educate yourself about your loved one's illness or disability. The more you know, the more confident and successful you will be as a caregiver!

Often times, caregivers neglect their own needs, believing that they should put their loved one first. Taking care of your own health and well-being is essential not only for yourself but also for your loved one. Remember, you must care for yourself first before you can truly be successful at caring for someone else. Self-care is one of the most forgotten steps for caregivers.

If you are feeling overburdened, never be afraid or embarrassed to ask for help. Sometimes doing something like taking a walk, meditating, enjoying a hobby, or reading a good book can help you feel in control again. Make sure you have a good support group. It could be other family members, friends, neighbors, or someone at your place of worship. There are also online caregiver support groups and other organizations that are specific to your loved one's illness or disability.

Take advantage of community services in your area. They may include senior centers, adult day care, home health aides, respite care, transportation services, or home-delivered meals. Sometimes the cost is covered by the care recipient's insurance plan or based on your ability to pay.

Caregiving can be a very emotional experience and can trigger things like guilt, anger, grief, and anxiety. It is important to accept and acknowledge these feelings. Having these kinds of emotions doesn't mean that you are a terrible person or that you don't care about your loved one. It only means that you are human! It is quite literally impossible to do it all yourself, which is why having some kind of support is so important. Taking care of your own needs is never a selfish act. As a caregiver, it is as important for you as it is for your loved one!

Even though caregiving is often an unnoticed and thankless job, most of us do it as an act of kindness, loyalty, and love! My first book, titled *Optimal Caregiving: A guide for managing senior health and well-being,* addresses concerns about senior care, nutritional needs, safety tips, healthy aging, and self-care for the caregiver. It is available on www.amazon.com as well as international bookstores.

Helpful Resources:

Alzheimer's Association
800-272-3900
www.alz.org

Eldercare Locator
800-677-1116
www.eldercare.gov

Family Caregiver Alliance
800-445-8106
www.caregiver.org

National Institute on Aging Information Center
800-222-2225
www.nia.hih.gov

SanGenWoman: The Heart of the Sandwich Generation
www.SanGenWoman.com

The Senior List
www.theseniorlist.com

United We Age
www.unitedweage.org

Veterans Administration
855-260-3274
www.caregiver.va.gov

Well Spouse Association
800-838-0879
www.wellspouse.org

Zentangle Inspired Art
www.TangledArtBoutique.com

Recommended Reading:

https://alzauthors.com

Brecht, Carole. *The Artistry of Caregiving: Letters to Inspire Your Caregiver Journey.* South Carolina: CreateSpace Independent Publishing Platform, 2016.

Cornish, Judy. *The Dementia Handbook: How to Provide Dementia Care at Home.* South Carolina: CreateSpace Independent Publishing Platform, 2017.

Lee, Jean. *Alzheimer's Daughter.* South Carolina: CreateSpace Independent Publishing Platform, 2014.

Marie, Lianna. *Everything You Need To Know About Caregiving For Parkinson's Disease: The Complete Guide for Anyone Caring for Someone with Parkinson's Disease.* South Carolina: CreateSpace Independent Publishing Platform, 2016.

Morris, Virginia. *How to Care for Aging Parents*, 3rd Edition. New York: Workman Publishing Company, 2014.

Sawatsky, Jarem. *Dancing with Elephants: Mindfulness Training For Those Living With Dementia, Chronic Illness or an Aging Brain (How to Die Smiling Series)* (Volume 1). Manitoba: Red Canoe Press, 2017.

REFERENCES

Barba, Christine. March 18, 2019. "What Is the Difference Between Dementia and Alzheimer's?" https://www.beingpatient.com/difference-between-dementia-and-alzheimers/

Bursack, Carol Bradley. "Surprising and gratifying moments in caregiving: people with dementia can have moments of clarity. www.eldercarelink.com/Alzheimers-and-Dementia/surprising-and-gratifying-moments-in-caregiving-people-with-dementia-can-have-moments-of-clarity.htm.

Dolhun, Rachel M.D. October 01, 2018. "Ask the MD: What Is Lewy Body Dementia?" https://www.michaeljfox.org/foundation/news-detail.php?ask-the-md-what-is-lewy-body-dementia.

Family Caregiver Alliance, National Center on Caregiving. "Caregiving 101: On Being a Caregiver." https://www.caregiver.org/caregiving-101-being-caregiver.

Mayo Clinic Staff. October 13, 2015. "Mental Illness, Symptoms & Causes." https://www.mayoclinic.org/diseases-conditions/mental-illness/symptoms-causes/syc-20374968.

Mayo Clinic Staff. June 30. 2018. "Parkinson's disease." https://www.mayoclinic.org/diseases-conditions/parkinsons-disease/symptoms-causes/syc-20376055.

National Alliance on Mental Illness. "Mental Health Conditions." https://www.nami.org/Learn-More/Mental-Health-Conditions.

Parkinson's Foundation. "Stages of Parkinson's." https://parkinson.org/Understanding-Parkinsons/What-is-Parkinsons/Stages-of-Parkinsons.

Parkinson's Foundation. "What is Parkinson's?" https://parkinson.org/understanding-parkinsons/what-is-parkinsons.

The Lewy Body Society, Shining a light on Lewy Body Dementia. "About LBD, Science." https://www.lewybody.org/about-lbd/science.

UCSF Memory and Aging Center, Weill Institute for Neurosciences. "Lewy Body Dementias." https://memory.ucsf.edu/lewy-body-dementias.

WebMD. "What is Parkinson's Disease?" https://www.webmd.com/parkinsons-disease/parkinsons-disease-overview#1.

ACKNOWLEDGMENTS

I sit in gratitude to all the many people who accompanied me on this life journey. Many of you have come and gone over the years, but to those who stayed, I will always be grateful. The creation of this book has literally taken a village!

Sometimes there are people in our lives who have a significant impact on who we are and the direction our paths take without ever knowing that they have done so. I want to acknowledge some of them here. Robin Ferderer, thank you for always being there and being a part of some of my fondest memories. Both you and your family have been with me through some of the best times and some of my worst, and you will never know the extent of what that has meant to me. You and Doug, as well as the Schiefelbein and Ferderer families, will always have a special place in my heart!

A heartfelt thank you to the many doctors, nurses, and staff members who guided and cared for my family. It would be impossible to name all of you, but you will always have my undying gratitude.

To my family members, friends, and peers from far and near, who have been a constant source of support, inspiration, and encouragement. Your presence has been invaluable to me!

Carol Landeis, a special thank you for being there to cheer me on and encouraging me with your always kind, yet honest opinions. Carole Brecht, thanks for sharing your wisdom, support, and guidance. I will always be grateful that our professional relationship blossomed into a beautiful friendship!

My loyalty, thanks, and appreciation to my wonderful husband and the love of my life, Randy. As both life partner and friend, you have helped me persevere through many of life's challenges and kept me sane. You are, and always will be, my rock! To my children Cory and Carisa, you are my life's greatest treasure and the truest source of unconditional love. Thanks for always having faith in me!

To my precious grandchildren, Alexa, Vincent, and Xander. You are my hope and vision for the future as you carry on the legacy of truth and wisdom for this family. I am so proud to be your grandma, and I hope you will always know how much you mean to me!

To my two very loving and loyal dogs, Zoey and Mylee. Thanks for being patient with me and for always being my constant companions. Especially when things are less than perfect!

Finally, to my father, Clifford "Jack," words cannot describe my deep gratitude for always believing in me, standing by me, and of course, for being a wonderful dad, grandfather and great-grandfather. I am so grateful to share this journey, and I certainly couldn't have made it this far without you. We will always make a great team. I love you!

To my readers: If you enjoyed my book, *In Search of Rainbows*, please take a moment to leave a review. It not only helps me but others as well. Thank you!

ABOUT THE AUTHOR

Susan Landeis is a writer, author, certified nutritionist, and a certified senior advocate. She has been a caregiver for her father and late mother for over a decade. Prior to this, she spent over twenty years working in the field of Health Information Management. Susan lives in the beautiful state of Colorado with her husband and two dogs. She has two adult children and three beautiful grandchildren.

Susan is the author of *Optimal Caregiving, A guide for managing senior health and well-being*. After struggling to manage her parents' growing health issues, she turned to natural healthcare and nutrition for answers. After seeing positive results, she felt inspired to write a book to help others who care for elderly loved ones.

As a senior advocate, Susan enjoys writing about her own personal experiences as well as other relevant topics, which include health and nutrition, caregiving, eldercare, and related subjects. She also spends her time blogging and advocates for causes close to her heart. When she isn't working on projects, Susan loves being in the great outdoors, traveling with her husband, and spending time with her beloved family.

To learn more and connect with Susan, you can visit her website at www.susanlandeis.com. Her first book, *Optimal Caregiving: A guide for managing senior health and well-being*, is available for purchase at www.amazon.com and international bookstores. You can also find the link on her website.

www.ingramcontent.com/pod-product-compliance
Lightning Source LLC
Chambersburg PA
CBHW021407290426
44108CB00010B/425